MANCHESTER UNITED

10 Seasons

at

Old Trafford

1984/85 to 1993/94

SEASON BY SEASON WRITE-UPS
Cliff Butler

EDITOR
Michael Robinson

CONTENTS

British Library Cataloguing in Publication Data
A catalogue record for this book is available from the British Library
ISBN 0-947808-42-6

Printed by Redwood Books, Kennet House, Kennet Way, Trowbridge, Wilts.

MANCHESTER UNITED CLUB FIRSTS

Originally formed in 1878 as Lancashire and Yorkshire Railway Company Newton Heath, the name was changed in 1892 to Newton Heath FC (which was the name of the company's main Manchester depot). The club played at a 'mud-heap' of a ground in North Street and, a founder member of the Football Alliance, joined the Football League in 1892 when the Alliance and the League merged. In 1893 they moved to Bank Street, Clayton, an equally 'salubrious' ground adjacent to a chemical works, and by 1902 went into liquidation. A local brewer, J.H. Davies, rescued the club, changed its name to Manchester United FC and upgraded the Bank Street ground.

After the club's F.A. Cup victory in 1909, Mr. Davies purchased a site several miles away (next to the Lancashire County Cricket Ground), and in 1910 began constructing the 'Old Trafford' which we know today. During the Second World War German bombers inflicted severe damage on the stadium and United were forced to share Manchester City's Maine Road ground for a number of years until, in 1949, the stadium was rebuilt.

In the late 1950's, the 'Busby Babes' carried all before them until the team was decimated by the 1958 'Munich disaster' in which the bulk of the first-team players lost their lives. As with the stadium, the 'phoenix' of Manchester United was, once again, forced to rise from the ashes and, through the dedication and skill of their management team, the club once more fought their was back to the forefront of the English soccer scene.

First F.A. Cup tie

Drawn against Higher Walton in the first qualifying round of the 1890/91 competition, Newton Heath won the tie 2-0 to earn a second qualifying-round tie against Bootle. Bootle, Everton's chief rivals for the Merseyside crown, won the game 1-0.

In the first qualifying round of the 1891/92 competition, Newton Heath met their local rivals Ardwick (Manchester City) and won 5-1. They went on to beat Heywood in the second round (3-2) but went out 4-3 to Blackpool in the final qualifying round.

Their first match in the competition proper was played on 21st January 1893 when (as a First Division side) they were no longer required to qualify! Blackburn Rovers, their Lancastrian opponents, won the tie 4-0.

First Football League match

Newton Heath were founder members of the Football Alliance in 1889 and remained in that competition until its amalgamation with the Football League in 1892 (when it became the Second Division). In fact, as the First Division was then increased in size, Newton Heath were elected straight into it, having being Alliance runners-up in the 1891/92 season. Their first fixture on 3rd September 1892 was away to Blackburn Rovers and the game ended in a 4-3 defeat. Five more fixtures were played before they recorded their first win - a thumping 10-1 victory over Wolverhampton Wanderers. Donaldson (who had scored four in the previous six games) and Stewart both picked up hat-tricks in a game which still remains United's biggest League victory. Ironically, 41 years later, Wolves inflicted United's equal heaviest defeat (7-0). They ended their first League season at the bottom of the First Division but won the test matches to remain in the top division until, in 1893/94, they finished bottom again and were relegated to the Second Division.

First Football League match as 'Manchester United'.

Their first fixture under their new name was played on 6th September 1902 and a single goal by Richards gave them a victory over Gainsborough Trinity, their Second Division opponents.

First Football League Championship.

In 1907/8, just two seasons after being promoted back from the Second Division, United romped to their first League Championship, winning by nine clear points from Aston Villa.

First F.A. Cup Final win

United experienced their first real success in the F.A. Cup in 1905/6 when they lost to Woolwich Arsenal in the semi-finals and, in 1908/9, they reached their first Final. The game was played at the Crystal Palace stadium and United beat their opponents, Bristol City, 1-0.

First F.A. Youth Cup win

Matt Busby's policy of promoting the development of young players was highlighted when, in 1953, the Manchester United youth team met Wolverhampton Wanderers in the first F.A. Youth Cup Final. United, fielding, amongst others, Duncan Edwards (who, in 1955 became the youngest-ever England international) won the home leg 7-1 and the tie 9-3 on aggregate.

Manchester United F.C. Winners of the F.A. Cup 1908-1909.

United went on to emphasize the brilliance of their young players by winning the next four F.A. Youth Cup Finals.

First European Competition

On 12th September 1956, Manchester United became the first English club to appear in the European Cup (Chelsea withdrew from the 1955/56 competition) and were drawn against the Belgian club RSC Anderlecht. The first leg was played in Belgium and United recorded an impressive 2-0 victory. In the home leg, Dennis Viollet scored United's first European hat-trick and Tommy Taylor scored another as United attained the first ever double-figure scoreline in the competition (10-0). United progressed to their first semi-final by beating Borussia Dortmund and Atletico Bilbao but then met the holders, Real Madrid. United lost the away leg 3-1 but were unable to pull back the deficit at Old Trafford and lost the tie 5-3 on aggregate.

First floodlit match at Old Trafford

This was played on 25 March 1957 between United and Bolton Wanderers in a Football League First Division match, which Bolton won 2-0.

The Munich Tragedy

The 1956/57 season saw the 'Busby Babes' romp to the League Championship by eight clear points and, representing England in the 1957/58 European Cup, got off to an excellent start by beating Shamrock Rovers 9-2 on aggregate. In the next round, United eliminated Dukla Prague 3-1 on aggregate and in the quarter-final beat Red Star Belgrade 5-4 on aggregate before disaster struck. Returning from Yugoslavia after drawing 3-3 to win the quarter-final tie on aggregate, United's plane crashed on take-off at Munich. Amongst others, eight players, including the brilliant Duncan Edwards, lost their lives and United's European Championship aspirations were crushed. In the semi-finals, AC Milan won 5-2 on aggregate against a hastily assembled team of reserves and new buys.

In 1958/59, UEFA, with a much applauded gesture towards United's heroism, offered them a place in the finals. The Football League and Football Association put considerable pressure on United, forcing them to refuse UEFA's kindness.

Sir Matt Busby, (pictured with daughter Sheena).

Though seriously injured in the Munich Tragedy, Sir Matt went on to manage United to European success in 1968.

First Football League Cup game

Manchester United were one of the few big clubs to compete in the first League Cup competition and on 19th October 1960 played their first fixture away to Exeter City. A goal by Dawson late in the game earned United a 1-1 draw and they won the replay 4-1. In the second round, United lost 2-1 at Bradford City.

First European Cup-Winner's Cup match

On 25th September 1963, United's first game in the competition was played away to the Dutch side Willem Tilburg 11 and ended in a 1-1 draw. In the home leg on 15th October 1963, Denis Law notched up their first hat-trick of the competition, as they won the game 6-1. In the next round their opponents were the holders, Tottenham Hotspur and United pulled back a 2-0 away leg deficit to win the tie 4-3 on aggregate before losing the semi-final to Sporting Lisbon.

First Fairs Cup match

On 23rd September 1964, United's first opponents in the competition were the Swedish club Djurgaarden. United drew the away game 1-1 but took the tie 7-2 on aggregate thanks, once more, to Denis Law who scored a hat-trick at Old Trafford. United then stormed through to the semi-finals against Ferencvaros but lost 2-1 in the play-off after drawing 3-3 on aggregate over the first two games.

Manchester United F.C. European Champions 1968.

First European trophy

In 1967/68 United once again faced Real Madrid in the semi-finals of the European Cup and, after winning the home leg by a single goal, played superbly at the Charmartin Stadium, to draw 3-3 and win the tie 4-3 on aggregate. United were fortunate indeed that the final was to be played at Wembley but, facing Eusebio's Benfica, could have hoped for easier opposition. The game was drawn 1-1 at the final whistle and United stormed ahead in extra-time to win 4-1. Scenes of great emotion followed the victory when Matt Busby, together with Bill Foulkes and Bobby Charlton (all survivors of the Munich disaster), saw their team achieve what fate had torn away in 1958.

First Football League Cup Final

The League Cup has not, over the years, proved to be a competition in which United have achieved much success. It was 1982/83 before they reached their first final; then, playing against Liverpool, the winners of the two previous competitions, they lost 2-1 after extra-time. United finally won the League Cup in 12th April 1992 when McClair scored to beat Nottingham Forest 1-0.

Matt Busby raises the European Cup after United's success in 1968.

SEASON 1984-85

This particular season will always be remembered for two of the worst tragedies football has ever suffered.

The horrific events which occurred at Heysel and Bradford have been documented elsewhere in the history books. They left the whole of football numb and in a state of total shock. May 1985 will go down as the darkest month that the game has ever endured.

As with most major disasters, it prompted the authorities to issue new legislation and in the case of the Heysel tragedy, UEFA swiftly slapped a ban on all English clubs from taking part in European Competition.

So that meant that United, who had triumphed in the F.A. Cup final, would not be allowed to participate in the European Cup Winners' Cup.

It was a desperately sad end all round to a season which had seen United carry off the F.A. Challenge Cup for the 6th time.

Everton, who had already clinched the League Championship, were United's opponents at Wembley in what was, by any standards, a dramatic final. Extra-time was required to separate the teams after normal time had ended with the Reds reduced to 10-men after Kevin Moran had become the first player to be sent off in the season's showpiece occasion.

The United defender had clumsily fouled Everton's Peter Reid, but many observers believed that a booking would have sufficed. As it was, the setback merely galvanised United into greater deeds and they went on to snatch the Cup and end Everton's hopes of the 'Double'. Norman Whiteside scoring the afternoon's only goal.

It was measure of compensation for the club after they had faded towards the end of the title race to finish in 4th position, fourteen points adrift of Everton, the champions.

United had enjoyed a reasonably comfortable run to the final. AFC Bournemouth were eliminated 3-0 in the third round and Coventry City defeated 2-1 in the fourth. Both those games being played at Old Trafford.

In the fifth round, United were drawn away to Blackburn Rovers. A tricky tie on the face of it, but United eased through with a 2-0 success.

Norman Whiteside was the Reds' hero in the sixth round as he helped himself to a hat-trick as West Ham United were ousted 4-2 at Old Trafford.

The semi-final against Liverpool provided, not one but two, stirring battles. The teams drew 2-2 at Goodison Park, but in the replay at Maine Road, United managed to get their noses in front in another tight contest to snatch a place at Wembley. Mark Hughes and Bryan Robson were United's scorers in a 2-1 win.

United's form in the League was generally of a high standard, but occasional slips meant that they were again destined to miss out on the main target.

United were involved in several high-scoring performances. Most notably at Old Trafford, where they put five past Newcastle United, West Ham United and Stoke City. Arsenal and Aston Villa were also in the firing-line; both clubs having four scored against them.

The Reds ended the season in fourth position, some fourteen points behind Everton, the Champions.

The Milk Cup campaign lasted for just three games. Burnley were easily dismissed from the competition in the second round. United winning 4-0 at Old Trafford and 3-0 at Turf Moor. But then United were shown the door by Everton, who won 2-1 at Old Trafford. That defeat coming just four days after the Toffees had given the Reds an almighty 5-0 mauling in a League fixture at Goodison Park.

The club's UEFA Cup campaign looked promising until they were surprisingly beaten on penalties, in the quarter-final, by little-known Hungarian side, Videoton.

In earlier rounds United had despatched Raba Vasas NTO Gyor (also from Hungary), Dutch side PSV Eindhoven and Dundee United.

Arthur Albiston ended the season at the top of United's appearance table with 57 outings from 60 games. Mark Hughes led the goalscorers' list with 25 in all competitions.

SEASON 1985-86

After eighteen years without a League title to celebrate, United's loyal and eminently patient supporters began to get more than a little excited during the opening weeks of the season.

They had waited a long time to see a glimmer of light at the end of the tunnel and early results hinted that the light was going to get brighter.

Reason for the unbridled exuberance? An incredible opening run of ten straight victories, which led to United being installed as hot favourites for the Championship. They were seemingly unbeatable as they reeled off a series of comprehensive successes.

And it wasn't just that they were winning, but they were winning in a style akin to that generally associated with successful United sides of the past.

Most notable of those opening victories were away at Arsenal and West Bromwich Albion. Both Arsenal Stadium and The Hawthorns had long been hoodoo grounds for United, and to snatch the points at those venues certainly provided extra cause for hope.

So, August and September passed with United perched proudly atop the Canon League Division One table with a virtually unblemished record of: Player 10, Won 10, Drawn 0, Lost 0, Goals For 27, Goals Against 3, Points 30.

No wonder the Reds' vast army of supporters were beginning to believe that Christmas had arrived early as United approached their 11th game of the season - against Luton Town at Kenilworth Road. Success against the Hatters would put United in the history books as having equalled Spurs' 1960 record of 11 consecutive wins from the start of the season.

Expectancy was high at the compact Bedfordshire ground, but ultimately it wasn't to be. United scored first through mark Hughes, but Brian Stein equalised for Luton and Tottenham Hotspur's unique place in the record books was preserved.

United remained unbeaten for a further five games before they suffered their first defeat. By then the season had reached early November and it was Sheffield Wednesday who claimed the distinction of lowering United's colours. it was also the beginning of the end for the Reds' title dream. They were never quite the same again after the 1-0 setback at Hillsborough. They won just two further games in the run-up to Christmas.

At the turn of the year they remained at the top of the table, but the chasing pack were starting to close in.

About that time rumours began to circulate regarding the future of star striker Mark Hughes. Talk was, that he was bound for Barcelona at the end of the season. The club confirmed they had given the Catalan giants first option on the Welsh International should he decide to move, but nothing was cut and dried.

Nevertheless, Hughes did decide to go at the season's close and all the talk about his possible move during the second half of the season certainly had an unsettling effect amongst the fans.

Ultimately, United finished fourth behind Liverpool, the champions, Everton and West Ham United. They had completed the season 12 points adrift of the Anfield Reds.

The F.A. Cup didn't really offer any solace. United going out to West Ham, 2-0, in a fifth round replay at Old Trafford. Earlier rounds saw United eliminate Rochdale and Sunderland.

The Milk Cup also brought United and the Hammers together, with the Reds winning a third round tie at Old Trafford by a goal to nil. However, the competition soon turned sour for United as they were knocked out in the very next round. Paul McGrath scored for the Reds, but Liverpool managed to fight back to take the tie 2-1 at Anfield.

United also participated in the Screen Sport Super Cup, a competition organised for those clubs who had qualified for Europe but unable to enter due to UEFA's ban following the Heysel Stadium disaster.

It was a largely disappointing tournament for United, who failed to win any of their four group matches.

They drew twice, 1-1 both times with Norwich City, and lost twice to Everton. The competition attracted a luke warm reception from the fans in that it was a poor second best to the excitement and thrills provided by a visit from one of the continent's top sides.

SEASON 1986-87

The frustration caused by United's failure to clinch the 1985-86 title after looking virtual certainties at one stage meant that the new season would begin with manager Ron Atkinson's performance under intense scrutiny.

Only another concerted tilt at the elusive championship would be enough to placate the fiercely ambitious 'Red Army'.

A good opening to the season was absolutely imperative to restore faith in the Atkinson regime, but that wasn't to happen. In fact, it's hard to imagine events being more unfavourable for the Reds' boss.

Three consecutive defeats heralded in the new campaign - away at Arsenal and home to West Ham United and Charlton Athletic - and as a result the team slumped to the foot of the table.

A 1-1 draw at Leicester and a more hopeful 5-1 home win over Southampton followed, but it was only a brief respite as two further reverses (away at Watford and Everton) kept United languishing at the 'wrong' end of the league table.

A slight improvement in fortune by October saw United elevated from the bottom three, but it wasn't enough to prevent United from parting company with Ron Atkinson early in November.

Ron Atkinson, the much respected manager whose failure to secure the Championship for United led to his dismissal. He has since gone on to manage Sheffield Wednesday and Aston Villa.

Ironically, the axe fell, not after a league defeat, but following the club's elimination from the League Cup.

United were well beaten, 4-1, by Southampton at The Dell and the following day Atkinson was summoned to Old Trafford to be informed that his contract had been terminated.

Ron Atkinson had been at the club for over six years, in which time he had led United to F.A. Cup triumph on two occasions.

His place, in what is arguably football's hottest seat, was promptly occupied by Alex Ferguson, the man who had enjoyed remarkable success with Scottish League Club, Aberdeen. Ferguson's appointment came within hours of Atkinson vacating the post.

In his time at Pittodrie, Ferguson had taken the club to unprecedented success on all fronts, with a string of titles and cup wins to his credit. Aberdeen also gained success in Europe when they defeated Real Madrid in Gothenburg to lift the 1983 European Cup Winners' Cup.

There was no denying that Alex Ferguson was arriving at Old Trafford with all the right credentials, but could he succeed where so many others had failed? Could he provide the winning formula to win the League title that United's vast army of supporters craved?

The answer to both those questions was, of course, 'Yes'. But it was to be a long and arduous road before he, and United, were to reach their goal.

As it was, the new boss didn't have to wait long before he was given a quick example of how great a task lay ahead of him. His very first game in charge, just two days after he had checked in at Old Trafford was at unfashionable Oxford United.

On the face of it an easy fixture with which to ease himself into the manager's chair. That's how it appeared, but the reality was quite different as United tumbled to a 2-0 defeat.

It was the first step along the road that was eventually to see United return to the pinnacle of English football.

United slowly eased themselves away from the relegation zone during the months that followed, but it was with a steady rather than spectacular blend of football that saw them consolidate their place in the top bracket. A status, which at one point had looked a little fragile.

The club eventually finished in a mid-table 11th position. And there was little comfort to be gleaned from their performance in the F.A. Cup. True, they knocked out Manchester City, 1-0 at Old Trafford, in the third round, and that to United supporters is always a welcome result.

But the glory was short-lived as the Reds tumbled out, in the next round, to Coventry City, the eventual winners of the trophy.

SEASON 1987-88

In preparation for his first full season as manager of Manchester United, Alex Ferguson made a couple of excursions into the transfer market.

The first signature he acquired was that of Arsenal and England defender, Viv Anderson. The tall, Nottingham-born player offered a wealth of experience at both club and International level.

Having netted Anderson, the Reds' boss moved his sights from defence to attack and focussed on his native city Glasgow to secure the services of Celtic's Brian McClair.

The former University student from Airdrie had been amongst the goals throughout his time at Parkhead and his eye for an opening would be needed if United were to make any inroads into the Merseyside domination of English football.

So, with the pre-season out of the way - including a four-match tour of Scandinavia - United opened the new league programme with a match against Southampton at the Dell.

Not the easiest of fixtures at any time, but United acquitted themselves well, scored twice through Norman Whiteside and gained a point. It was an acceptable opening day performance.

A goalless draw with Arsenal at Old Trafford was the next match on the agenda and then the Reds reeled off three successive victories. Watford and Chelsea were beaten at Old Trafford with the other win coming on an outing at Charlton Athletic. It all added up to a promising start and a sound platform on which to build.

This mini-run of success was followed up by another couple of draws, 0-0 at Coventry City and 2-2 with Newcastle United at Old Trafford, but then came the season's first defeat; 1-2 at Everton.

Happily, the defeat at Goodison Park didn't upset the momentum which then seemed to be developing and they proceeded to remain unbeaten in their next seven League games.

Then came another defeat, 1-2 at Wimbledon, but still the record looked good, with just those two defeats coming in the opening sixteen games.

But was it to be good enough? For whilst United were winning and drawing matches in almost equal quantities, Liverpool, at the top of the table, remained unbeaten and they had already opened up what appeared to be an unassailable lead.

The Reds' boss was under no illusions, he knew that the team was far from finished and in mid December he again brought out the club's cheque book to pay Norwich City a sizeable sum for central defender Steve Bruce.

The one-time Wallsend schoolboy player had made his name with Gillingham before moving to Carrow Road where he built up a reputation for being reliable in defence more than handy in attack when going forward for set pieces.

Bruce quickly established himself in the Reds' defence as the team gradually eased themselves into second place in the table.

Their league form held up well and in any other season they would probably have been in with an excellent chance of taking the honour. But not this particular season. Why? Because, Liverpool were simply in a class of their own. The Anfield giants completed the season having lost just two games and with 90 points, a new record.

United had not been disgraced, but there was no catching the men from Merseyside. And they had to be content with runners-up spot, some nine points behind their great rivals from the other end of the East Lancashire Road.

The final outcome didn't really give United's adoring fans any great pleasure. To them there was no glory in being second best to Liverpool, but at least it showed that Alex ferguson was on the right track. And he could also take some comfort from the season's performance of Brian McClair, the striker he'd snapped up from Celtic.

The Scottish international more than repaid Ferguson's faith in his ability by snatching 31 goals in all competitions - 24 of them in the League.

The cup competitions failed to provide any glory as United were eliminated from both the Littlewoods Cup and the F.A. Cup at the fifth round stage. Oxford United were responsible for ending the Reds' interest in the Littlewoods, whilst Arsenal did the same in the senior cup tournament.

SEASON 1988-89

Alex Ferguson returned to his former club, Aberdeen, for his one major signing of the 1988 close season.

He had, on becoming manager at Old Trafford, inherited the considerable talents of Aberdeen old-boy Gordon Strachan, and shortly after the close of the 1987-88 season he moved quickly to take another Pittodrie favourite, Jim Leighton, to Old Trafford.

The Reds' boss didn't require any lengthy scouting reports on the big Scottish International. He had been Leighton's boss for many years and anyway the Johnstone-born custodian had long been regarded as a goalkeeper of the highest calibre.

There was a mood of optimism as the new season approached, but the question was, could United go one better than the runners-up spot of the previous campaign.

Well, from early on in the League programme there seemed little chance that this was to be United's year. Too many games were drawn, too few ended in victory and with three months of the season having lapsed United were hovering in mid-table.

There were few really heart-warming moments during the first half of the campaign and inconsistency wasn't helped when several players were sidelined through injury.

But in the midst of what was a pretty uninspiring spell came a performance which stood out like a beacon.

New Year's Day 1989 brought United's arch-rivals, Liverpool, to Old Trafford. The Mersey-Reds weren't enjoying the domination of the previous season's title race, but nevertheless they were a good few places above United when they arrived to help usher in the New Year.

A big crowd packed into Old Trafford in the hope of seeing United record a morale-boosting victory. They weren't to be disappointed.

The first half passed without any goals being scored and a large slice of the second period also ticked away in the same way. But then, in the 70th minute, John Barnes delighted the Liverpool fans at the Scoreboard End by scoring the game's opening goal.

The remainder of the ground fell into silence, but they didn't have to wait long for their turn to lift the roof. Within a minute, Brian McClair had grabbed the equaliser and Old Trafford was transformed into a cauldron of noise and colour.

The Red hordes were beside themselves, but there was better to come. Four minutes later, and United were in front thanks to a goal from Mark Hughes. Shortly after that, Russell Beardsmore struck to crash in United's third past Liverpool's Mike Hooper.

Liverpool couldn't believe it and United's followers were also finding hard to taking what they were witnessing. The visitors had started the game as favourites and yet here they were battling to keep United at bay.

United, and their fans, were elated, but typical of this roller-coaster season, the very next day they travelled north to take on Middlesbrough at Ayresome Park and they went down to a single goal from Peter Davenport, the former Old Trafford striker.

Having already lost interest in the Littlewoods Cup - going out in the third round at Wimbledon - United's remaining hopes of landing a trophy lay in the F.A. Cup.

The third round brought Queens Park Rangers to Old Trafford and they succeeded in holding United to a goalless draw. The replay at Loftus Road was also a tight affair and went to extra-time before the teams trooped from the field having drawn again, this time 2-2.

Happily, for United, they won the toss to stage the second replay and they also won the tie when Rangers were beaten 3-0 at Old Trafford.

Oxford United were despatched with some ease in the fourth round and then United squeezed past AFC Bournemouth - after a replay - to book their place in the sixth round.

United were awarded with a plum home tie against Nottingham Forest, but they couldn't use it to their advantage and they were beaten 0-1 before 55,040 fans. It was Old Trafford's biggest gathering of the entire season.

Meanwhile, the Reds continued to struggle to find decent form in the League and they ended the season in a disappointing 11th position.

SEASON 1989-90

Well into his third year at Old Trafford and manager Alex Ferguson must have been wondering what he had got himself into.

Perhaps, even he, with his marvellous record of success at Aberdeen was beginning to think that the task at United was going to be harder than he thought it might be.

One thing was for certain and that was that he wasn't going to leave a stone unturned in his search for the winning formula.

The 1989-90 season was going to give him plenty of sleepless nights, but ultimately it would be seen as a major watershed in the history of a great football club.

In his quest to put United back at the top of the pile he embarked on the biggest spending spree the club had ever seen.

The close season saw two midfield players move to Old Trafford. England international Neil Webb was transferred from Nottingham Forest and he was joined by Norwich City's Mike Phelan. The total outlay for these two players amounted to something in excess of £2.25m but it wasn't by any means the end of the manager's buying session.

The early weeks of the season saw him further dent the Old Trafford coffers with multi-million pound deals which secured the services of Middlesbrough's Gary Pallister, Paul Ince from West Ham United and Southampton's Danny Wallace.

A huge amount of money had been spent, but the benefit wasn't immediately apparent. The opening weeks of the season still left a great deal to be desired and the fans dreams that the days may be just around the corner turned to nightmares in late September when the Reds were hammered 5-1 by Manchester City at Maine Road.

The team had slumped into the relegation zone and even at this early stage of the season there were whispers of crisis amongst some of the club's supporters.

A 3-0 home defeat by Tottenham Hotspur saw United tumble out of the Littlewoods Cup in the third round.

But there was a measure of improvement in the League and they steadily began to ascend the table into a more comfortable position. It was, however, a short-lived change of direction for in the weeks running up to Christmas the team again found themselves slipping into the First Division's lower reaches.

Newspaper talk about crisis began to increase and it was suggested that should United fail to make any impact in the F.A. Cup then it would be again time to start looking around for a new manager.

It was a harrowing time for Alex Ferguson and he must have thought that the gods were against him when United were drawn to travel to Nottingham Forest in the F.A. Cup third round. The City Ground could hardly be described as United's favourite away venue, but the tie was to prove a turning point in the club's long history.

It was a tense, nervy match, but it all turned out well in the end after Mark Robins had headed United into the fourth round with the game's only goal early in the second half.

The next round took them to Hereford United, where a late Clayton Blackmore goal did the trick. A 3-2 win over Newcastle United at St. James's Park ensured a place in the sixth round and then Brian McClair scored the winner against Sheffield United at Bramall Lane to book a last-four slot.

The semi-final saw United and Oldham Athletic battle through two fabulous matches before the Reds clinched their place in the final the a 2-1 replay win.

League form during this time had barely held its head above water, but at least United were safe from the drop and they were clear to concentrate on trying to win the F.A. Cup for the 7th time.

United faced Crystal Palace in the final, and after drawing the original game 3-3 the Reds carried off the Cup thanks to a second half goal from Lee Martin in the replay.

It was a wonderful night for Manchester United, a wonderful night for Alex Ferguson and it placed the club on the threshold of a spell of unprecedented success.

SEASON 1990-91

When the elite of European football is the topic of conversation it is a sure bet that Manchester united will be mentioned at some point.

The Mighty Reds from Old Trafford stand shoulder to shoulder with the continent's great clubs such as Real Madrid, AC Milan, Barcelona, Liverpool, Ajax and Bayern Munich.

Arguably, United are the biggest name of them all, but in terms of major European silverware they lag far behind all the other great names listed above.

And, until the triumph of lifting the European Cup Winners' Cup in 1991, they

Manchester United and Liverpool are pictured together after the 1-1 draw in the 1990 Charity Shield.

could look back on just one major honour in the continent's three top competitions. That great moment when Bobby Charlton hoisted aloft the European Cup at Wembley, after defeating Portugal's Benfica was just a distant memory for older fans. Those of more tender years could only read of that glorious night of watch videos of the occasion.

So, the winning of the European Cup Winners' Cup not only restored United to a position at the forefront of European football, it also gave United's younger fans an opportunity to sample the excitement of a triumph at the very highest level.

The Road to Rotterdam started with a tie against little-known Hungarian side, Pecsi Munkas. Drawn to play at home in the first leg, United didn't exactly set Old Trafford on fire with their display, but they did at least win the game, 2-0, to put themselves in a handy position to finish the job in Hungary. And that they did with Brian McClair scoring in the 77th minute to seal Pecsi's fate.

The second round saw United paired with Wrexham, the Welsh Cup holders, and again the Reds were drawn to play at home in the first leg. The lads from North Wales weren't really expected to cause United too much trouble and in the end it did prove to be a comfortable passage for United. A 3-0 win at Old Trafford in front of 29,405 fans was followed by a 2-0 victory at The Racecourse.

United, it seemed, were managing to avoid the competition's big-boys such as Juventus and Sampdoria from Italy, Spain's Barcelona and the Soviet Union's Dynamo Kiev. And their luck held when the quarter-final draw was made as they came out of the bag with France's Montpellier.

The club from the South of France could hardly be described as their nation's most famous club, but nevertheless they gave United a scare by snatching a 1-1 draw at Old Trafford in the first leg. Many people changed their opinion after watching the first leg and suddenly the match in France took on a very different look.

Montpellier were confident that they could upset the odds, but United had other ideas and a brilliant performance - perhaps the best of the entire season - saw United through with a 2-0 win. Just three hours of football was all that stood between United and a place in a major European final for the first time in 23 years. And the team they had to get past to reach that final was Legia Warsaw. The Polish side had dismissed crack Italian's Sampdoria in the quarter finals so they were treated with the greatest of respect when United travelled to the Polish capital in early April.

A draw in Warsaw would be brilliant, with the second leg still to be played in Manchester, but United did better than that, in fact, much better than that, despite going behind early on. They recovered from that setback to score through Brian McClair, Mark Hughes and Steve Bruce to place one foot firmly in the final.

If anything, the return leg was something of an anti-climax. The Old Trafford crowd projected a feeling that the game was a formality, and that's just what it was. Legia never really threatened to spoil the party and United seemed content to see the game through without too much exertion.

The match ended 1-1 with Lee Sharpe scoring for United, and the club's first European final since the days of Bobby Charlton, George Best, Pat Crerand, Bill Foulkes etc. was confirmed.

Barcelona, one of Europe's most battle-hardened clubs was the side which United would meet in the final at the Feyenoord Stadium in Rotterdam. It was expected to be a close contest and that is a pretty accurate way of describing the match.

The first half passed without a goal, but after the break it was a very different story. United scored twice - both from Mark Hughes - but Barca pulled one back through Ronald Koeman with eleven minutes to go.

It was a tense last few minutes but United held on to take the trophy and send their huge army of fans into ecstasy.

It was a happy ending to a season which saw United lose the League Cup Final, 0-1 to Sheffield Wednesday at Wembley, go out of the F.A. Cup at the fifth round stage at Norwich and finish a disappointing sixth in the Division One table. One place and three points behind neighbours Manchester City.

SEASON 1991-92

Will United ever win the League title again? That question must have been on the lips of many Reds' fans after United had again thrown away what looked to be another excellent opportunity to win the championship.

The Reds were involved in what amounted to a virtual season-long race to the winning post with great rivals Leeds United. For most of the time United had the edge over the Elland Road outfit, but when it really mattered, in the closing weeks of the season, United found the strain too much. And Leeds were left to pick up the famous old trophy whilst the Reds could only reflect on what was another missed chance.

The season had started really well for United as they remained unbeaten in their opening dozen games. Sadly, it was a case of unlucky thirteen as they suffered their first defeat in an away match at Hillsborough. Ironically, it was also Sheffield Wednesday who had thrown a spanner in the works when United had looked title-bound back in season 1985-86.

Leeds, meanwhile, were keeping in step with United as a tantalising contest between two of football's fiercest rivals began to take shape.

Happily, for United, the 2-3 defeat at Hillsborough hadn't dented morale too severely and they quickly recovered to put together another unbeaten run of eight league games without reverse.

During that spell United began to take on the look of a side that was capable of winning the title. Their defence had developed a mean streak which by Christmas had restricted opposing teams to a miserly 14 goals in 21 matches. And that included two rare occasions when three goals were leaked. One of those games was the 2-3 defeat at Hillsborough, whilst the other, against Oldham Athletic at Boundary Park passed by almost unnoticed because in the

Ryan Giggs hailed by some as 'The Next George Best', established himself as a first team regular in the 1991/92 Season.

same match United crashed six past the Latics.

There was no doubting that United's new found confidence in defence was bolstered in the knowledge that the last-line was Peter Schmeichel, the giant Danish international goalkeeper, who had been signed from Brondby during the previous summer.

Manager Alex Ferguson had also added the not inconsiderable talents of Queens Park Rangers and England defender Paul Parker to the Old Trafford payroll at the same time and there was no question that the Red's regular back-four of Paul Parker, Steve Bruce, Gary Pallister and Denis Irwin was the rock on which the title challenge was being mounted.

Then, the first day of the New Year brought an amazing result as United were humbled, 1-4, by mid-table Queens Park Rangers - a side that had never before won a game on United's home ground. The shock defeat didn't immediately rock the boat, but from then on the title challenge was never really quite as steady as it had been.

Another nine games passed before United would again taste defeat, but of those nine league fixtures, five were drawn.

Clayton Blackmore in action against Liverpool's David Burrows.

However, United still looked to be in with a marvellous chance of snatching the title as the race moved into the final straight. It was well within their grasp with less than a month of the programme to run. United's destiny remained in their own hands, for having 36 games - six to play - United were a point behind Leeds, but they had two games in hand.

Ultimately, it didn't prove to be of any advantage. United lost three of those matches, at home to Nottingham Forest and away to West Ham and Liverpool. Leeds, on the other hand, had kept plugging away and they claimed their reward on Sunday 26th April after United's failure to beat Liverpool in the Anfield cauldron put the Elland Road side four points in the clear with only one game each left to compete.

Alex Ferguson, his players and their legions of supporters were understandably crestfallen. Midway through the season they were all supremely confident that the barren years were about to end, and yet here they were again thinking of what might have been.

Having said that, the season wasn't a total failure. United won the Rumbelows League Cup for the first time by defeating Nottingham Forest, 1-0, at Wembley, and they also added the European Super Cup to the collection after the European Champions, Red Star Belgrade, had been beaten 1-0 at Old Trafford - Brian McClair scoring the winning goal in both triumphs.

There had been plenty to cheer, lots of brilliant football to admire, but United would have gladly swapped their two cup successes for that elusive League championship.

SEASON 1992-93

Twenty-six years without a League championship is a very long, long time, but for a club of Manchester United's stature it's an eternity.

Fans of the club has long rejoiced in claiming that the Reds are the 'Greatest Football Club in the World', but it's mighty hard to back up those bold words with hard facts when your team hasn't taken its nations' top prize for more than a quarter of a century.

United's failure to win the title for such a long time had not gone unnoticed by the supporters of all United's rivals. They had taken sheer delight in taunting Reds' fans for years about their team's shortcomings. So it's hardly surprising that it was an overwhelming feeling of relief, as well as delight, that greeted United's first championship since 1967.

The celebrations which followed were volcano-like. Twenty-six years of pent-up frustration was released in a carnival of joy and excitement. It had all come right at long last, the long wait was over, but the opening week of the season

A pensive Alex Ferguson watches United battle for Championship points.

didn't provide any indication that glory was just a matter of months away.

The first day of the season took United across the Pennines for a match against Sheffield United at Bramall Lane. It's always nice to get off on the right foot, but United didn't, the Blades won the match 2-1. Alright, they had failed to launch the season in the ideal way, but it was only one match and nothing to get too despondent about.

That wasn't the feeling four days later after Everton had been entertained at Old Trafford. The Toffees crushed United 3-0 and immediately the talk turned to the season already being a lost cause.

Two games, two defeats and all hope was gone, at least that's what some fans would have had you believe. True, there hadn't been much to inspire confidence, but two poor performances from a 42-match programme is a little early to start worrying unduly.

The following Saturday saw Ipswich Town at Old Trafford and a slight change of fortune was the outcome of the game as United took their first point of the season from a 1-1 draw. Nothing to get over excited about, but they had to start their recovery somewhere.

Two days later they were at the Dell and it was from then on that the challenge for the inaugural F.A. Premier League title got underway. United had never really looked on Southampton as one of the favourite away grounds, but on this occasion it produced the launch-pad for their assault on the big prize.

Dion Dublin, the big striker who had been signed from Cambridge United shortly before the start of the season, was given his first start in a United shirt. And he justified the manager's decision in giving him his debut by grabbing the winner with two minutes to go. It was a perfect start for the tall target man, but delight was to turn to tragedy for him in United's very next home game.

Crystal Palace were the visitors and although United won the game 1-0 to continue their revival - they had beaten Nottingham Forest at the City Ground four days earlier - the joy of winning was reduced after it was confirmed that Dublin had broken a leg. He had been stretchered from the field late in the first half. It was a cruel blow for the likeable lad who was just starting his career at Old Trafford.

A couple of 2-0 victories followed - at home to Leeds United and away at Everton - and as a result United started to ascend the table. They found themselves in the top three with 'unlikely' contenders, Blackburn Rovers and Norwich City, above them.

The Reds had strung together five straight victories, but the hope that they generated was soon to evaporate as the team ran into a glut of drawn games. The points were shared in the next five games and a slide down the table soon followed. Even worse was to come when a home match with Wimbledon was lost 0-1, and a similar result came out of an away fixture at Aston Villa.

United's tumble down the league had halted at 10th place and all talk about the championship looked over for another year. Arsenal were in top spot early in November, eight points ahead of United. But what made things worse for United fans was the knowledge that arch-rivals Manchester City were also higher placed in the table.

All looked very bleak, for not only was United's league form suffering, but they had also been eliminated from both the UEFA Cup (by Torpedo Moscow) and the Coca-Cola Cup by Aston Villa. But then, just when doom and gloom was about to set in, the course of the season changed for the better.

Wins over Oldham Athletic at Old Trafford and away at Arsenal put a smile back on Red faces and then, in early December, manager Alex Ferguson pulled off a masterstroke which was to make all the difference to United's dream of glory.

An informal telephone call with Howard Wilkinson, the Leeds United boss, led to Eric Cantona being mentioned in the conversation, and within hours the French international was exchanging the white of Leeds for the red of Manchester. It was an amazing piece of transfer activity which took the whole of football by surprise and whilst it delighted United's supporters, equally it angered their counterparts at Elland Road.

One thing is for certain, and that is that the signing of Cantona gave United a whole new dimension. There was an immediate upturn in fortune and the Reds ended the year with two great results. A 3-3 draw against Sheffield Wednesday at Hillsborough (after being 0-3 behind at one stage) and a 5-0 demolition of Coventry City at Old Trafford. They had moved up into second place in the Premier League table and there was talk again about United being serious contenders for the crown.

It had all been seen before. United had threatened to win the League on numerous occasions since 1967, so could this tilt be taken seriously, or was it just another false dawn?

The answer to both those posers came during the second half of the season as United emerged as the team to be reckoned with. Aston Villa, managed by former United boss Ron Atkinson, became the only real danger to United's aspirations and ultimately they faded from view in much the same way United had in the chase with Leeds, the previous season.

The second half of the campaign saw United beaten on just two occasions, at Ipswich Town and Oldham Athletic. Their consistency during the final run proved to be decisive as they rattled a sequence of seven consecutive wins. It was a blistering pace which left Villa in United's wake.

So, the first F.A. Premier League title had been won by Manchester United. Many people couldn't believe what had happened. It took a long time to sink in, but it didn't prevent the fans from celebrating in traditional fashion.

It had been a long time coming.

SEASON 1993-94

Hailed as the team of the 90's and installed as favourites for pretty well every trophy, United didn't disappoint those who had lavished compliments upon them as they concluded a memorable season in glorious fashion.

The memories of glory days long past came flooding back as the team which Alex Ferguson built became only the sixth club in English football history to complete the highly-coveted League & Cup double. All round it was a brilliant season for the club. They made the running in the title race from the start and they were strongly tipped to become the first club ever to collect all three domestic trophies in one season.

Some pundits scoffed at the idea and said it was impossible. No club, not even United at their scintillating best, could achieve that. And those who predicted that the Reds would fail in the attempt were proved right, but United went agonisingly close to pulling it off.

Starting a new season as reigning champions for the first time since the Busby era, United were universally acclaimed as a side of the highest quality. They had taken the 1993 title with a brand of football which bore all the hallmarks of classic United sides of the past. Just winning the title would have been enough to end all those years of misery. But the long overdue honour had been achieved with a flourish. It had been achieved with flamboyant and creative football which put the icing on the cake.

Many football experts confidently expected United to put up a strong defence of their precious title. Hardly a bold prediction after the way United had captured the imagination of neutral followers with their classy football. Nevertheless, it must have been music to Alex Ferguson's ears. Only three short years before, his career at Old Trafford had been given the last rites by a section of the football press. The adulation and praise heaped upon the club was a wonderful tribute to Ferguson's managerial ability. But he didn't allow it to cloud his judgement and he certainly wasn't about to rest on his laurels.

The job of keeping a major club at the top is never ending and with the new season in mind he made one significant foray into the transfer market to secure the services of Roy Keane, Nottingham Forest's Republic of Ireland international. Ferguson had long admired the talents of the Cork-born midfield man and he was forced to splash out a massive fee to clinch the deal.

The arrival of Keane to join United's already impressive first team squad must have looked ominous for the rest of the Premiership. The brilliant Reds had stormed to the title with a team of all talents and the belief was that they could only get better. And United were about to prove that correct.

They started their defence with a brilliant opening run of five wins in the first six games. The odd-one out being a draw with Newcastle United at Old Trafford. A brilliant 2-1 away win at Villa Park was included in that opening burst. it was a great result over their rivals of the previous season and it was achieved with football of the highest quality. The pundits were already purring and the season was less that a fortnight old.

A 0-1 defeat by Chelsea at Stamford Bridge in early September halted their progress, but it was only a blip as they headed towards a second successive championship.

United were in Budapest the following Wednesday to begin their European Cup campaign against Kispest Honved. It was the first time they had appeared in the competition since 1969, and they got off to an excellent start by defeating the Hungarian champions 3-2. The second leg at Old Trafford, a fortnight later, didn't present too much of a problem as United moved comfortably into round two with a 2-1 win.

Back on the league front they were merrily moving along with a string of impressive performances and they had also progressed in the Coca-Cola Cup despite losing the second round, first leg match against Stoke City at the Victoria Ground. The Potters won the match 2-1, but United turned the tie round in the return to take the tie 3-2 on aggregate.

The next round of the European Cup pitched United in with little-fancied Turkish side, Galatasaray. The Istanbul club were not short on experience in Europe, but they weren't expected to cause United too much trouble. They weren't expected to, but they did and they gave United a two-goal start before fighting back to record an excellent 3-3 draw at Old Trafford.

The surprise outcome left United with a precarious mission in the second leg. United had to win or be involved in an unlikely draw of 4-4 or more. The Turks would be happy with a goalless draw, and that's just what they got in the frantic atmosphere of the Ali Sami Yen Stadium in Istanbul.

It was a disappointing end to the Reds' first jaunt in the Champions' Cup for two decades, but at least they had plenty to look forward to on the domestic front.

Their league defence went pretty well to plan as they piled up win after win to keep Kenny Dalglish's Blackburn Rovers at bay. Only a poor spell in March, during which Eric Cantona was sent off in two successive matches - at Swindon and Arsenal - was there a hint of a waiver. And whilst Rovers did brilliantly to close the gap, United held their nerve to finish the season strongly with four wins and a draw from their last five outings.

In the Coca-Cola Cup they put out Leicester City, Everton, Portsmouth and Sheffield Wednesday before meeting Aston Villa at Wembley. It was United's third final in the competition in four years, but it wasn't to be their day.

Former United boss, Ron Atkinson, was the manager of Sheffield Wednesday when they defeated United in the 1991 League Cup final and he was shown to have all the answers again as Villa took the trophy with a 3-1 win.

So, United's dream treble lay in ruins, but they were not going to sit around getting depressed. By this time they had already reached the F.A. Cup semi-final, having beaten Sheffield United, Norwich City, Wimbledon and Charlton Athletic along the way. The classic 'double' was still very much on the cards.

The semi-final saw them paired with neighbours Oldham Athletic and United needed two games - just as they had when the teams met in 1990 - to clinch their place at Wembley. It wasn't easy, and but for an equalising goal from Mark Hughes in the final minute of extra time in the original tie at Wembley, United would have been out. A 4-1 win followed at Maine Road, but Oldham made them fight all the way.

United were now in sight of the double, a feat only previously achieved by Aston Villa and Preston North End in the last century and by Spurs, Arsenal and Liverpool since the last World War. They were to face Chelsea - the only team to have twice beaten United in the league. Gavin Peacock having scored the winning goal in 1-0 wins at both Stamford Bridge and Old Trafford.

Nonetheless, United were favourites against the West London side who were appearing in their first final since 1970. The Blues, of course, fancied their chances and in the first half of a rain-soaked final were the better side. United, it seemed, had it all to do. The second half was a very different story as the Reds cruised to a record-equalling 8th cup win - Spurs, the only other club with that record - by the resounding score of 4-0. Two penalties - both converted by Eric Cantona - helped to comprise that impressive total with Mark Hughes and brian McClair also getting into the scoring act.

The celebrations which followed were predictably euphoric. After years of threatening to become a big-time club, united had at last arrived. This was their sixth major trophy - two championships, two F.A. Cup wins, one League Cup and one European Cup Winners' Cup - in five seasons. It was a great moment for everyone connected to the club.

Alex Ferguson was quick to dedicate the season to the memory of Sir Matt Busby, who had passed away four months earlier. The great man would have been delighted to see the club he made into an institution carry off the double, playing football in the way he would have loved.

Manchester United had placed their flag at the summit once more.

Bryan Robson, United's 'Captain Marvel' who left at the end of the 1993/94 season to become manager of Middlesbrough.

In 13 years at the Club, he made 345 League appearances and scored 74 goals.

1984-85

#						Result	Scorers	Attendance
1	Aug	25	(h)	Watford	D	1-1	Strachan (pen)	53,668
2		28	(a)	Southampton	D	0-0		22,183
3	Sep	1	(a)	Ipswich T	D	1-1	Hughes	20,434
4		5	(h)	Chelsea	D	1-1	Olsen	48,298
5		8	(h)	Newcastle U	W	5-0	Hughes, Moses, Olsen, Strachan 2 (1 pen)	54,915
6		15	(a)	Coventry C	W	3-0	Robson, Whiteside 2	18,482
7		22	(h)	Liverpool	D	1-1	Strachan (pen)	56,638
8		29	(a)	West Brom A	W	2-1	Robson, Strachan (pen)	26,401
9	Oct	6	(a)	Aston Villa	L	0-3		37,132
10		13	(h)	West Ham U	W	5-1	Brazil, Hughes, McQueen, Moses, Strachan	47,559
11		20	(h)	Tottenham H	W	1-0	Hughes	54,516
12		27	(a)	Everton	L	0-5		40,769
13	Nov	2	(h)	Arsenal	W	4-2	Hughes, Robson, Strachan 2	32,279
14		10	(a)	Leicester C	W	3-2	Brazil, Hughes, Strachan (pen)	23,840
15		17	(h)	Luton T	W	2-0	Whiteside 2	42,776
16		24	(a)	Sunderland	L	2-3	Hughes, Robson	25,405
17	Dec	1	(h)	Norwich C	W	2-0	Hughes, Robson	36,635
18		8	(a)	Nottingham F	L	2-3	Strachan 2 (1 pen)	25,902
19		15	(h)	QPR	W	3-0	Brazil, Duxbury, Gidman	36,134
20		22	(h)	Ipswich T	W	3-0	Gidman, Robson, Strachan (pen)	35,168
21		26	(a)	Stoke C	L	1-2	Stapleton	21,013
22		29	(a)	Chelsea	W	3-1	Hughes, Moses, Stapleton	42,197
23	Jan	1	(h)	Sheffield W	L	1-2	Hughes	47,638
24		12	(h)	Coventry C	L	0-1		35,992
25	Feb	2	(h)	West Brom A	W	2-0	Strachan 2	36,681
26		9	(a)	Newcastle U	D	1-1	Moran	31,798
27		23	(a)	Arsenal	W	1-0	Whiteside	48,612
28	Mar	2	(h)	Everton	D	1-1	Olsen	51,150
29		12	(a)	Tottenham H	W	2-1	Hughes, Whiteside	42,918
30		15	(a)	West Ham U	D	2-2	Robson, Stapleton	16,674
31		23	(h)	Aston Villa	W	4-0	Hughes 3, Whiteside	40,941
32		31	(a)	Liverpool	W	1-0	Stapleton	34,886
33	Apr	3	(h)	Leicester C	W	2-1	Robson, Stapleton	35,590
34		6	(h)	Stoke C	W	5-0	Hughes 2, Olsen 2, Whiteside	42,940
35		9	(a)	Sheffield W	L	0-1		39,380
36		21	(a)	Luton T	L	1-2	Whiteside	10,320
37		24	(h)	Southampton	D	0-0		31,291
38		27	(h)	Sunderland	D	2-2	Moran, Robson	38,979
39	May	4	(a)	Norwich C	W	1-0	Moran	16,006
40		6	(h)	Nottingham F	W	2-0	Gidman, Stapleton	43,334
41		11	(a)	QPR	W	3-1	Brazil 2, Strachan	20,483
42		13	(a)	Watford	L	1-5	Moran	20,047

FINAL LEAGUE POSITION: 4th in Division One

Appearances

Sub. Appearances

Goals

Bailey	Duxbury	Albiston	Moses	Moran	Hogg	Robson	Strachan	Hughes	Brazil	Olsen	Whiteside	Muhren	McQueen	Gidman	Stapleton	Garton	McGrath	Blackmore	Pears	
1	2	3	4	5	6	7	8	9	10*	11	12									1
1	2	3	4	5	6	7	8	9	10	11										2
1	2	3	4	5	6	7	8	9	10*	11	12									3
1	2	3	4	5	6	7	8	9		11	10									4
1	2	3	4	5	6	7	8	9		11	10									5
1	2	3	4	5	6	7	8	9		11	10									6
1	2	3	4	5*	6	7	8	9		11	10	12								7
1	2	3	4	5	6	7	8	9	10	11										8
1	2	3	4	5	6		7	9	10	11			8							9
1	2	3	4		6	7	8	9	10	11			5							10
1		3	4	5	6	7	8	9	10	11				2						11
1		3	4	5*	6	7	8	9	10	11				2	12					12
1		3	4	5	6	7	8	9		11				2	10					13
1		3	4		6	7	8	9	10	11	12			2	5					14
1	6	3	4			7*	8	9		11	10		5	2	12					15
1		3	4			7	8	9		11	10	12	5	2	6					16
1		3	4			7	8	9		11	10		5	2	6					17
1	2		4			7	8		10			11	5		9	6	3			18
1	6	3	4			7	8		10	11			5	2	9					19
1	6	3	4			7	8	9		11			5	2	10					20
1	6	3	4			7	8*	9	12	11			5	2	10					21
1	2	3	4			7	8*	10		11			5		9	6				22
1	2	3	4			7	8	9	10	11			5		6					23
	2	3	4			7*	8		10	11	12		5		9		6		1	24
		3	4	5	6		8	9		11	10			2			7		1	25
		3	4	5	6		8	9	10	11*				2	12		7		1	26
1	4	3		5*	6		8	9		11	12			2	10		7			27
1	4	3			6	7	8	9		11				2	10		5			28
1	4	3			6	7		9		11	8			2	10		5			29
1	4	3			6	12	7	9		11	8*			2	10		5			30
1		3			6	7	8	9		11	4			2	10		5			31
1		3			6	7	8	9		11	4			2	10		5			32
1		3			6	7	8	9		11	4			2	10		5			33
1	12	3			6	7*	8	9		11	4			2	10		5			34
	4*	3			6	7	8	9	12	11				2	10		5		1	35
1		3			6	7		9		11	4	8		2	10		5			36
1	12	3			6	7	8	9		11	4			2	10*		5			37
1	12	3			6	7	8	9	10	11	4			2*			5			38
1		3			6	7	8	9		11	4			2	10		5			39
1		3	5*	6			8		10	11	4	12		2	9		7			40
1	7	3		6*			8		10	11	4	12		2	9		5			41
1	7	3		6			8	9		11	4*	12		2	10		5			42
38	27	39	26	19	29	32	41	38	17	36	23	7	12	27	21	2	23	1	4	
	3			1				3	4	5					3					
	1		3	4	9	15	16	5	5	9			1	3	6					

33

1985-86

1	Aug	17	(h)	Aston Villa	W 4-0	Whiteside, Hughes 2, Olsen	49,743
2	.	20	(a)	Ipswich T	W 1-0	Robson	18,777
3		24	(a)	Arsenal	W 2-1	Hughes, McGrath	37,145
4		26	(h)	West Ham U	W 2-0	Hughes, Strachan	50,773
5		31	(a)	Nottingham F	W 3-1	Hughes, Barnes, Stapleton	26,274
6	Sep	4	(h)	Newcastle U	W 3-0	Stapleton 2, Hughes	51,102
7		7	(h)	Oxford U	W 3-0	Whiteside, Robson, Barnes	51,820
8		14	(a)	Manchester C	W 3-0	Robson (pen), Albiston, Duxbury	48,773
9		21	(a)	West Brom A	W 5-1	Brazil 2, Strachan, Blackmore, Stapleton	25,068
10		28	(h)	Southampton	W 1-0	Hughes	52,449
11	Oct	5	(a)	Luton T	D 1-1	Hughes	17,454
12		12	(h)	QPR	W 2-0	Hughes, Olsen	48,845
13		19	(h)	Liverpool	D 1-1	McGrath	54,492
14		26	(a)	Chelsea	W 2-1	Olsen, Hughes	42,485
15	Nov	2	(h)	Coventry C	W 2-0	Olsen 2	46,748
16		9	(a)	Sheffield W	L 0-1		48,105
17		16	(h)	Tottenham H	D 0-0		54,575
18		23	(a)	Leicester C	L 0-3		22,008
19		30	(h)	Watford	D 1-1	Brazil	42,181
20	Dec	7	(h)	Ipswich T	W 1-0	Stapleton	37,981
21		14	(a)	Aston Villa	W 3-1	Blackmore, Strachan, Hughes	27,626
22		21	(h)	Arsenal	L 0-1		44,386
23		26	(a)	Everton	L 1-3	Stapleton	42,551
24	Jan	1	(h)	Birmingham C	W 1-0	Gibson C	43,095
25		11	(a)	Oxford U	W 3-1	Whiteside, Hughes, Gibson C	13,280
26		18	(h)	Nottingham F	L 2-3	Olsen 2 (1 pen)	46,717
27	Feb	2	(a)	West Ham U	L 1-2	Robson	22,642
28		9	(a)	Liverpool	D 1-1	Gibson C	35,064
29		22	(h)	West Brom A	W 3-0	Olsen 3 (2 pens)	45,193
30	Mar	1	(a)	Southampton	L 0-1		19,012
31		15	(a)	QPR	L 0-1		23,407
32		19	(h)	Luton T	W 2-0	Hughes, McGrath	33,668
33		22	(h)	Manchester C	D 2-2	Gibson C, Strachan (pen)	51,274
34		29	(a)	Birmingham C	D 1-1	Robson	22,551
35		31	(h)	Everton	D 0-0		51,189
36	Apr	5	(a)	Coventry C	W 3-1	Gibson C, Robson, Strachan	17,160
37		9	(h)	Chelsea	L 1-2	Olsen (pen)	45,355
38		13	(h)	Sheffield W	L 0-2		32,331
39		16	(a)	Newcastle U	W 4-2	Robson (pen), Hughes 2, Whiteside	31,840
40		19	(a)	Tottenham H	D 0-0		32,357
41		26	(h)	Leicester C	W 4-0	Stapleton, Hughes, Blackmore, Davenport (pen)	38,840
42	May	3	(a)	Watford	D 1-1	Hughes	18,414

FINAL LEAGUE POSITION: 4th in Division One

Appearances

Sub. Appearances

Goals

Bailey	Gidman	Albiston	Whiteside	McGrath	Hogg	Robson	Moses	Hughes	Stapleton	Olsen	Duxbury	Strachan	Brazil	Barnes	Moran	Blackmore	Garton	Gibson C	Dempsey	Turner	Wood	Gibson T	Sivebaek	Davenport	Higgins	
1	2	3	4	5	6	7	8*	9	10	11	12															1
1	2*	3	4	5	6	7		9	10	11	12	8														2
1		3	4	5	6	7		9	10	11	2	8														3
1		3	4	5	6	7		9	10	11	2	8														4
1		3	4	5	6	7		9	10		2	8*			12	11										5
1		3	4	5	6	7		9	10*		2	8			12	11										6
1		3	4	5	6	7		9	10*		2	8			12	11										7
1		3	4	5	6	7		9	10*		2	8			12	11										8
1		3	4	5	6	7		9			2	8*	10		12	11										9
1		3	4*	5		7	8	9	10		2				12	11	6									10
1		3	4	5		7	8	9	10		2					11	6									11
1		3	4	5		7	8	9	10		2					11	6									12
1		3	4	7	6		8*	9	10	11	2				12	5										13
1		3	4	7	6		8	9	10		2				11	5										14
1		3	4	7	6		8	9	10						11	5	2									15
1	2	3	4	5		7*	8	9	10						12	11	6									16
1	2	3	4	5			8	9	10			7				11	6									17
1	2	3*	4	7	6			9	10	11		8			12	5										18
1	2		4	7	6			9	10	11		8			12	5*		3								19
1	2		4	5	6			9*	10	11		8			12			3	7							20
	2		4	5				9	10*	11		8			12	7	6	3		1						21
1	2		4	5				9	10	11		8				7	6	3								22
1	2		4	5	6			9	10	11*		8				7		3				12				23
	2	3	4	5*				9	10			8			12	7	6	11		1						24
1	2	3	4					9	10			8			5	7	6	11								25
1	2	3	4					9	10		7	8			5		6	11								26
1	2	3	4	5		7*		9	10			8			6			11						12		27
	2	3	4	5				9	12	11*		8			6			10		1				8	7	28
	2*	3		5				9	10	11		7			6		4	8		1				12		29
		3		5		7		9	10	11*	2	8			6		4			1				12		30
		3		5				9	7		2	8			6		4*	11		1		12		10		31
		3	4	5				9	12	11	2	8			6*			7		1				10		32
		3	4	5				9	12		2	8				11*		7		1				10	6	33
	2	3	4	5		7		9	12			8				11*				1				10	6	34
	2	3	4	5		7		9	12			8				11				1				10*	6	35
	2	3	4	5		7		9	12			8				11*				1				10	6	36
	2	3		5		7		9	12	11	4	8*								1				10	6	37
	2	3		5		7		9		11	4									1		12	8	10*	6	38
	2	3	4	5		7		9	10							11	6			1			8*	12		39
	2	3	4	5				9	10	12	7					11	6			1			8*			40
	2	3	4*	5				9	10	12	7					11	6			1			8			41
		3	4	5	6			9	10	12	7					11	2			1			8*			42
25	24	37	37	40	17	21	4	40	34	25	21	27	1	12	18	12	10	18	1	17		2	2	11	6	
									7	3	2	1		10	1	1						1		5	1	
		1	4	3		7		17	7	11	1	5		3	2	3		5						1		

35

1986-87

1	Aug	23	(a)	Arsenal	L	0-1		41,362
2		25	(h)	West Ham U	L	2-3	Stapleton, Davenport	43,306
3		30	(h)	Charlton A	L	0-1		37,544
4	Sep	6	(a)	Leicester C	D	1-1	Whiteside	16,785
5		13	(h)	Southampton	W	5-1	Olsen (pen), Davenport, Stapleton 2, Whiteside	40,135
6		16	(a)	Watford	L	0-1		21,650
7		21	(a)	Everton	L	1-3	Robson	25,843
8		28	(h)	Chelsea	L	0-1		33,340
9	Oct	4	(a)	Nottingham F	D	1-1	Robson	34,828
10		11	(h)	Sheffield W	W	3-1	Davenport 2 (1 pen), Whiteside	45,890
11		18	(h)	Luton T	W	1-0	Stapleton	39,927
12		26	(a)	Manchester C	D	1-1	Stapleton	32,440
13	Nov	1	(h)	Coventry C	D	1-1	Davenport	36,948
14		8	(a)	Oxford U	L	0-2		13,545
15		15	(a)	Norwich C	D	0-0		22,634
16		22	(h)	QPR	W	1-0	Sivebaek	42,235
17		29	(a)	Wimbledon	L	0-1		12,112
18	Dec	7	(h)	Tottenham H	D	3-3	Whiteside, Davenport 2 (1 pen)	35,957
19		13	(a)	Aston Villa	D	3-3	Davenport 2, Whiteside	29,205
20		20	(h)	Leicester C	W	2-0	Gibson C, Stapleton	34,180
21		26	(a)	Liverpool	W	1-0	Whiteside	40,663
22		27	(h)	Norwich C	L	0-1		44,610
23	Jan	1	(h)	Newcastle U	W	4-1	Jackson P (og), Whiteside, Stapleton, Olsen	43,334
24		3	(a)	Southampton	D	1-1	Olsen	20,409
25		24	(h)	Arsenal	W	2-0	Strachan, Gibson T	51,367
26	Feb	7	(a)	Charlton A	D	0-0		15,482
27		14	(h)	Watford	W	3-1	McGrath, Davenport (pen), Strachan	35,763
28		21	(a)	Chelsea	D	1-1	Davenport (pen)	26,516
29		28	(h)	Everton	D	0-0		47,421
30	Mar	7	(h)	Manchester C	W	2-0	Reid (og), Robson	43,619
31		14	(a)	Luton T	L	1-2	Robson	12,509
32		21	(a)	Sheffield W	L	0-1		29,888
33		28	(h)	Nottingham F	W	2-0	McGrath, Robson	39,182
34	Apr	4	(h)	Oxford U	W	3-2	Davenport 2, Robson	32,443
35		14	(a)	West Ham U	D	0-0		23,486
36		18	(a)	Newcastle U	L	1-2	Strachan	32,706
37		20	(h)	Liverpool	W	1-0	Davenport	54,103
38		25	(a)	QPR	D	1-1	Strachan	17,414
39	May	2	(h)	Wimbledon	L	0-1		31,686
40		4	(a)	Tottenham H	L	0-4		36,692
41		6	(a)	Coventry C	D	1-1	Whiteside	23,407
42		9	(h)	Wimbledon	W	3-1	Blackmore, Duxbury, Robson	35,179

FINAL LEAGUE POSITION: 11th in Division One

Appearances

Sub. Appearances

Goals

Turner	Duxbury	Albiston	Whiteside	McGrath	Moran	Strachan	Blackmore	Stapleton	Davenport	Gibson C	Olsen	Gibson T	Sivebaek	Hogg	Robson	Moses	Barnes	Walsh	O'Brien	Garton	Gill	Bailey	Wood	
1	2	3	4	5	6	7	8	9	10	11*	12													1
1	2	3	4	5	6	7	8	9	10	11*	12													2
1	2	3	4*	5	6	7	8	9	10		11	12												3
1	8	3	4	5		7		9	12	11	10*		2	6										4
1		3	4	5	6	8*		9	10	11	12		2		7									5
1		3		5	6		8	9	10		11		2		7	4								6
1		3	4*	5	6	8		9	10		12		2		7	11								7
1		3	4	5	6	8		9	10		12		2		7	11*								8
1		3	4	5	6	8		9	10		11		2		7									9
1		3	4	5		8		9	10				2	6	7	11								10
1		3	4	5		8*		9	10			12	2	6	7	11								11
1		3	4	5				9	10				2	6	7	8	11							12
1		3	4	5		8		9	10	11			2	6	7*	12								13
1	2	3	5*	4		7		9	10		12			6		8	11							14
1	3		5	12		8		9	10	7			2*	6		4	11							15
1	3		5		12	8		9	10	7			2	6		4	11*							16
1	3		5	6		8		9	10	7			2		12	4	11*							17
1		3	9	5*	6	8		12	10		11		2		7	4								18
		3	9		5	8		12	10*		11		2	6	7	4		1						19
			9		5	8		12	10	3	11		2	6	7			1	4*					20
	6		4		5	8		9	10	3	11		2		7			1						21
	6		4			8		9	10	3	11		2		7*			1	12	5				22
1	7	9*		6		8		12	10	3	11		2			4	5							23
1	2					6	8		9	12	3	11	10			4	5		7*					24
1	3*		4	12	6	8	7	9			11	10	2				5							25
1	4			6		8		9	12	3	11	10*	2		7		5							26
1	4			5	6	8		12	9	3	11	10			7				2*					27
	2		4	5	6	8		12	9	3	11*	10			7							1		28
	2		4	5	6	11			9*	3	10			8	7		12					1		29
	4		9	5	6	8*			12	3	10		2		7		11					1		30
	4		9	5	6	8			12	3*	10		2		7		11					1		31
	3		9	5	6	8			10	11	12				7				4	2*		1		32
	6	12	10	5				9		3			2		7	8		1	4				11*	33
	6	12		5				9	11	3			2		7	8		1	4				10*	34
	2	12		5	6	8		9	11	3	10				7*	4		1						35
	2		10	5	6	8		12	11	3	9*					4		1	7					36
	7	3*	10	5	6	8		12	9	11			2			4		1						37
	2	3	9	5	6	8			10	11			12		7	4*		1						38
	2	3		5	6	8		12	9	11	10				7	4*		1						39
	4		10	5	6	8	12			3	11	9	2*		7			1						40
	4	3	9	5	6	8*	12		10	11					7			1	2					41
	4	3	9*	5	6		8		10	11	12				7			1	2					42
23	32	19	31	34	32	33	10	25	34	24	22	12	27	11	29	17	7	14	9	9	1	5	2	
	3		1	1	1	2	9	5		6		4	1		1	1			3					
	1		8	2		4	1	7	14	1	3		1		1	7								

37

1987-88

1	Aug	15	(a)	Southampton	D 2-2	Whiteside 2	21,214
2		19	(h)	Arsenal	D 0-0		42,890
3		22	(h)	Watford	W 2-0	McGrath, McClair	38,582
4		29	(a)	Charlton A	W 3-1	McClair, Robson, McGrath	14,046
5		31	(h)	Chelsea	W 3-1	McClair, Strachan, Whiteside	46,478
6	Sep	5	(a)	Coventry C	D 0-0		27,125
7		12	(h)	Newcastle U	D 2-2	Olsen, McClair (pen)	45,137
8		19	(a)	Everton	L 1-2	Whiteside	38,439
9		26	(h)	Tottenham H	W 1-0	McClair (pen)	47,601
10	Oct	3	(a)	Luton T	D 1-1	McClair	9,137
11		10	(a)	Sheffield W	W 4-2	Robson, McClair 2, Blackmore	32,779
12		17	(h)	Norwich C	W 2-1	Davenport, Robson	39,345
13		25	(a)	West Ham U	D 1-1	Gibson	19,863
14		31	(h)	Nottingham F	D 2-2	Robson, Whiteside	44,669
15	Nov	15	(h)	Liverpool	D 1-1	Whiteside	47,106
16		21	(a)	Wimbledon	L 1-2	Blackmore	11,532
17	Dec	5	(a)	QPR	W 2-0	Davenport, Robson	20,632
18		12	(h)	Oxford U	W 3-1	Strachan 2, Olsen	34,709
19		19	(a)	Portsmouth	W 2-1	Robson, McClair	22,207
20		26	(a)	Newcastle U	L 0-1		26,461
21		28	(h)	Everton	W 2-1	McClair 2 (1 pen)	47,024
22	Jan	1	(h)	Charlton A	D 0-0		37,257
23		2	(a)	Watford	W 1-0	McClair	18,038
24		16	(h)	Southampton	L 0-2		35,716
25		24	(a)	Arsenal	W 2-1	Strachan, McClair	29,392
26	Feb	6	(h)	Coventry C	W 1-0	O'Brien	37,144
27		10	(a)	Derby Co	W 2-1	Whiteside, Strachan	20,016
28		13	(a)	Chelsea	W 2-1	Bruce, O'Brien	25,014
29		23	(a)	Tottenham H	D 1-1	McClair	25,731
30	Mar	5	(a)	Norwich C	L 0-1		19,129
31		12	(h)	Sheffield W	W 4-1	Blackmore, McClair 2, Davenport	33,318
32		19	(a)	Nottingham F	D 0-0		27,598
33		26	(h)	West Ham U	W 3-1	Strachan, Anderson, Robson	37,269
34	Apr	2	(h)	Derby Co	W 4-1	McClair 3, Gibson	40,146
35		4	(a)	Liverpool	D 3-3	Robson 2, Strachan	43,497
36		12	(h)	Luton T	W 3-0	McClair, Robson, Davenport	28,830
37		30	(h)	QPR	W 2-1	Bruce, Parker (og)	35,733
38	May	2	(a)	Oxford U	W 2-0	Anderson, Strachan	8,966
39		7	(h)	Portsmouth	W 4-1	McClair 2 (1 pen), Davenport, Robson	35,105
40		9	(h)	Wimbledon	W 2-1	McClair 2 (1 pen)	28,040

FINAL LEAGUE POSITION: 2nd in Division One   Appearances

Sub. Appearances

Goals

Walsh	Anderson	Duxbury	Moses	McGrath	Moran	Robson	Strachan	McClair	Whiteside	Olsen	Albiston	Davenport	Gibson	Hogg	Garton	Blackmore	O'Brien	Graham	Turner	Bruce	Martin	#
1	2	3	4*	5	6	7	8	9	10	11†	12	14										1
1	2	3	4	5	6	7	8	9	10	11												2
1	2	3	4	5	6	7	8*	9	10	11†	14	12										3
1	2	3	4	5	6	7	8*	9	10	11†		14	12									4
1	2	7	4	5	6		8	9	10	11	3*		12									5
1	2	7	4	5	6		8	9	10	11†	3*	14	12									6
1	2	3	4	5	6	7	8	9	10	11*		12										7
1	2	3	4	5		7	8†	9	10	11		14			6*	12						8
1	2*	6		5		7	8†	9	10	11		14	3		4	12						9
1		6		5		7	8	9	10	11			3		4	2*	12					10
1		4		5	6*	7	8†	9	10	11		14	3		2	12						11
1		4		5	12	7		9	10	11		8	3		2*	6†	14					12
1	2	4		5	6	7	8*	9		11		10	3		12							13
1	2	4			6	7	12	9	10*	11		8	3		5							14
1	2	4			6*	7	8	9	10	11		12	3		5							15
1	2	3*	4		6	7		9	10	11	12				5	14	8†					16
	2	4		5		7	8	9		11			3	10			6		1			17
	2	4		5		7*	8	9	10	11		12	6	3					1			18
	2	6		5		7	8	9	10	11*		12	3						1	4		19
12	2	6†		5		7	8	9	10	14		11	3*						1	4		20
	2	6	12	5		7	8*	9	10†	11		14	3						1	4		21
	2	5	6*			7	8	9		11†		10	3			14	12		1	4		22
	2	6	5†			7	8	9	10		3*	12	11				14		1	4		23
	2	8	6	5†		7	12	9		11		10	3*				14		1	4		24
	2	3				7	8	9	10	11				6		5*	12		1	4		25
	2	3				7	8	9	10	11		12		6		5*			1	4		26
	2	3*				7	8	9	10	11†	12	14		6		5			1	4		27
	2					7		9	10		3	8	11*	6	12	5			1	4		28
	2†	3					12	9	10	14		7	11	6*		8	5		1	4		29
		3*			6	7	8	9		12		10	11			2	5		1	4		30
		5				7	8	9		11*		10	3	6		2	12		1	4		31
	2	5			14			9	7	8		10	11*	6†		3	12		1	4		32
	2	6	5			7	8*	9		12		10	11			3			1	4		33
	2	6	5†			7	8	9		12		10*	11	4		3	14		1			34
	2	6*	5			7	8	9	14	12		10	11			3†			1	4		35
	2	6	5			7	8	9		12		10	11*			3			1	4		36
	2	6	5			7	8	9		11		10				3*	12		1	4		37
	2*	6	5			7	8	9		11		10	3			12			1	4		38
	2†	6	5*			7	8	9		11		10	3	12		14			1	4		39
	2	6*	5			7	8	9				10	11			3			1	4	12	40
16	30	39	16	21	20	36	33	40	26	30	5	21	26	9	5	15	6	1	24	21		
	1		1	1	1	3			1	7		6	13	3	1	1	7	11	1			
	2	2				11	8	24	7	2		5	2			3	2			2		

39

1988-89

#	Month	Date		Opponent		Score	Scorers	Attendance
1	Aug	27	(h)	QPR	D	0-0		26,377
2	Sep	3	(a)	Liverpool	L	0-1		42,026
3		10	(h)	Middlesbrough	W	1-0	Robson	40,422
4		17	(a)	Luton T	W	2-0	Davenport, Robson	11,010
5		24	(h)	West Ham U	W	2-0	Davenport, Hughes	29,941
6	Oct	1	(a)	Tottenham H	D	2-2	Hughes, McClair	29,318
7		22	(a)	Wimbledon	D	1-1	Hughes	12,143
8		26	(h)	Norwich C	L	1-2	Hughes	36,998
9		30	(a)	Everton	D	1-1	Hughes	27,005
10	Nov	5	(h)	Aston Villa	D	1-1	Bruce	44,804
11		12	(a)	Derby Co	D	2-2	Hughes, McClair	24,080
12		19	(h)	Southampton	D	2-2	Robson, Hughes	37,277
13		23	(h)	Sheffield W	D	1-1	Hughes	30,867
14		27	(a)	Newcastle U	D	0-0		20,350
15	Dec	3	(h)	Charlton A	W	3-0	Milne, McClair, Hughes	31,173
16		10	(a)	Coventry C	L	0-1		19,936
17		17	(a)	Arsenal	L	1-2	Hughes	37,422
18		26	(h)	Nottingham F	W	2-0	Milne, Hughes	39,582
19	Jan	1	(h)	Liverpool	W	3-1	McClair, Hughes, Beardsmore	44,745
20		2	(a)	Middlesbrough	L	0-1		24,411
21		14	(h)	Millwall	W	3-0	Blackmore, Gill, Hughes	40,931
22		21	(a)	West Ham U	W	3-1	Strachan, Martin, McClair	29,822
23	Feb	5	(h)	Tottenham H	W	1-0	McClair	41,423
24		11	(a)	Sheffield W	W	2-0	McClair 2	34,820
25		25	(a)	Norwich C	L	1-2	McGrath	23,155
26	Mar	12	(a)	Aston Villa	D	0-0		28,332
27		25	(h)	Luton T	W	2-0	Milne, Blackmore	36,335
28		27	(a)	Nottingham F	L	0-2		30,092
29	Apr	2	(h)	Arsenal	D	1-1	Adams (og)	37,977
30		8	(a)	Millwall	D	0-0		17,523
31		15	(h)	Derby Co	L	0-2		34,145
32		22	(a)	Charlton A	L	0-1		12,056
33		29	(h)	Coventry C	L	0-1		29,799
34	May	2	(h)	Wimbledon	W	1-0	McClair	23,368
35		6	(a)	Southampton	L	1-2	Beardsmore	17,021
36		8	(a)	QPR	L	2-3	Bruce, Blackmore	10,017
37		10	(h)	Everton	L	1-2	Hughes	26,722
38		13	(h)	Newcastle U	W	2-0	McClair, Robson	30,379

FINAL LEAGUE POSITION: 11th in Division One

Appearances

Sub. Appearances

Goals

Manchester United appearance/scorer grid (players × matches).

Leighton	Blackmore	Martin	Bruce	McGrath	McClair	Robson	Strachan	Davenport	Hughes	Olsen	O'Brien	Anderson	Duxbury	Garton	Sharpe	Beardsmore	Robins	Donaghy	Gibson	Milne	Gill	Wilson	Maiorana	Whiteside	Brazil	Match
1	2	3	4	5	6	7	8	9*	10	11	12															1
1	3		4	5*	9	7	8†	14	10	11		2	6	12												2
1	3		4	5	9	7		8	10	11			6	2												3
1	3		4	5	9	7		8	10	11			6	2												4
1	2		4		9	7	8	11	10	12			6	5†	3*	14										5
1			4	5	9	7	8	11*	10	12		14	6	2†	3											6
1	2		4		9	7	8*	11†	10				6	5	3	12	14									7
1	2		4		9	7	8	11*	10	12			6	5	3											8
1	3		4		9	7	8*		10	11		14		5	2			6†	12							9
1	2		4		9	7	8		10	11		5	12					6	3*							10
1	3		4		9	7	8		10	12				5*	2	11		6								11
1	3		4		9	7	8		10						2	11*		6		5	12					12
1	3†		4		9	7	8*		10						2	11		6		5	12	14				13
1	3	12	4		9	7			10						2	11†	14	6		8*	5					14
1	5	3	4		9	7	8		10						2			6		11						15
1	5	3	4		9	7	8		10						2*	11		6		14	12†					16
1	5*	2†	4		9	7	8		10					3		14		6		11	12					17
1		2	4		9	7	8		10					3		5		6		11						18
1	2*		4	12	9	7	8†		10					3		5	14	6		11						19
1			4	5	9	7			10					3		8*	14	6		11	2†	12				20
1	8	2	4		9				10					3		5*		6		11†	7	12	14			21
1	5	3	4		9	7	8*		10				12					6		11	2					22
1	5	2	4	12	9	7	8†		10					3*			14	6		11						23
1	5	3	4	2	9	7	8		10*				12					6		11						24
1	2†	12	4	5	9	7	8		10					3			14	6		11*						25
1	12	3†	4	5	9	7	8		10					11	2*		14	6								26
1	3	2	4	5	9	7			10							8*		6		11		12				27
1	3	12	4	5*	9	7			10			2				8		6		11†	14					28
1	14	12	4	5	9	7			10			2				8†		3					11*	6		29
1	11		4	5*	9	7			10			2				8		3			12			6		30
1		3	4	5	9				10			2†	12			8*	7	6						14	11	31
1			4	5	9	7			10			2				8	12	3		11*				6		32
1	11*		4	5	9	7			10			2				8	12	3						6		33
1	11		4	5	9	7			10			2				8		3			12			6*		34
1	11*		4	5	9	7†			10			2	12			8		3					14	6		35
1	5	11	4		9				10			2		3*		8	12	6			7					36
1	5*	11	4		9				10			2†		3		8	12	6			7			14		37
1	5†	3	4		9	7			10			2		14		8	12	6		11*						38
38	26	20	38	18	38	34	21	7	38	6	1	5	16	13	19	17	1	30	1	19	4		2	6		
	2	4		2				1		4	2	1	2	1	3	6	9		1	3	5	4	4		1	
	3	1	2	1	10	4	1	2	14						2					3	1					

41

1989-90

1	Aug	19	(h)	Arsenal	W 4-1	Bruce, Hughes, Webb, McClair	47,245
2		22	(a)	Crystal Palace	D 1-1	Robson	22,423
3		26	(a)	Derby Co	L 0-2		22,175
4		30	(h)	Norwich C	L 0-2		39,610
5	Sep	9	(a)	Everton	L 2-3	McClair, Beardsmore	37,916
6		16	(h)	Millwall	W 5-1	Hughes 3, Robson, Sharpe	42,746
7		23	(a)	Manchester C	L 1-5	Hughes	43,246
8	Oct	14	(h)	Sheffield W	D 0-0		41,492
9		21	(a)	Coventry C	W 4-1	Bruce, Hughes 2, Phelan	19,605
10		28	(h)	Southampton	W 2-1	McClair 2	37,122
11	Nov	4	(a)	Charlton A	L 0-2		16,065
12		12	(h)	Nottingham F	W 1-0	Pallister	34,182
13		18	(a)	Luton T	W 3-1	Wallace, Blackmore, Hughes	11,141
14		25	(h)	Chelsea	D 0-0		47,106
15	Dec	3	(a)	Arsenal	L 0-1		34,484
16		9	(h)	Crystal Palace	L 1-2	Beardsmore	33,514
17		16	(h)	Tottenham H	L 0-1		36,230
18		23	(a)	Liverpool	D 0-0		37,426
19		26	(a)	Aston Villa	L 0-3		41,247
20		30	(a)	Wimbledon	D 2-2	Hughes, Robins	9,622
21	Jan	1	(h)	QPR	D 0-0		34,824
22		13	(h)	Derby Co	L 1-2	Pallister	38,985
23		21	(a)	Norwich C	L 0-2		17,370
24	Feb	3	(h)	Manchester C	D 1-1	Blackmore	40,274
25		10	(a)	Millwall	W 2-1	Wallace, Hughes	15,491
26		24	(a)	Chelsea	L 0-1		29,979
27	Mar	3	(h)	Luton T	W 4-1	McClair, Hughes, Wallace, Robins	35,327
28		14	(h)	Everton	D 0-0		37,398
29		18	(h)	Liverpool	L 1-2	Whelan (og)	46,629
30		21	(a)	Sheffield W	L 0-1		33,260
31		24	(a)	Southampton	W 2-0	Gibson, Robins	20,510
32		31	(h)	Coventry C	W 3-0	Hughes 2, Robins	39,172
33	Apr	14	(a)	QPR	W 2-1	Robins, Webb	18,997
34		17	(h)	Aston Villa	W 2-0	Robins 2	44,080
35		21	(a)	Tottenham H	L 1-2	Bruce (pen)	33,317
36		30	(h)	Wimbledon	D 0-0		29,281
37	May	2	(a)	Nottingham F	L 0-4		21,186
38		5	(h)	Charlton A	W 1-0	Pallister	35,389

FINAL LEAGUE POSITION: 13th in Division One

Appearances

Sub. Appearances

Goals

Leighton	Duxbury	Blackmore	Bruce	Phelan	Donaghy	Robson	Webb	McClair	Hughes	Sharp	Martin	Graham	Pallister	Robins	Anderson	Beardsmore	Ince	Wallace	Maiorana	Milne	Brazil	Gibson	Sealey	Bosnich	No.
1	2	3	4	5	6	7	8	9	10	11*	12														1
1	2	3	4	5	6	7	8	9	10	11															2
1	2	6	4	5		7	8	9	10	11	3*	12													3
1	2	3†	4	5		7*	8	9	10	11	12		6	14											4
1	2*	8	4	5	7			9	10	11	3†		6		12	14									5
1	12		4†	5	3	7		9	10	11			6		2	14	8*								6
1	4			5	3			9	10	12			6		2	7*	8	11							7
1	2*		4	5	3	7		9	10	14	12		6				8	11†							8
1	12		4	5	2	7		9	10	11†	3		6				8*		14						9
1		12	4	5	2	7		9	10	11	3		6				8*								10
1		12	4	5	2†	7		9	10	11*	3		6				8	14							11
1		2	4	5		7		9	10	12	3		6				8	11*							12
1		2	4	5		7		9	10		3		6				8	11							13
1	12	2	4	5		7		9	10		3*		6			14	8	11†							14
1		2*	4	5		7		9	10		3		6			12	8	11							15
1		14	4	5†		7		9	12	10*	3		6			2	8	11							16
1		14	4*	5		7		9	10	3			6		12	2†	8	11							17
1		2	4	5		7		9	10	12	3		6				8	11*							18
1	12	7†	4	5				9	10	11	3*		6	14	2		8								19
1		7	4	5				9	10	12	3		6	11	2		8*								20
1	12	8†	4	5				9	10	7*	3		6	11	2	14									21
1	12	8*	4	5				9	10		3		6	11	2	7†					14				22
1		14	4	5†				9	10		3		6	7	2	12	8*	11							23
1	8	7		5	4*			9	10		3		6	14	2	12		11†							24
1	8	7†		5				9	10		3		6	14	2*	4		11		12					25
1	7*		4	5	14			9	10		3		6		2†	12	8	11							26
1			4	5				9	10		3		6	7	2	12	8	11*							27
1	2	14	4	5				9	10*		3		6	7†		12	8	11							28
1	12	7	4	5				9	10		3		6		2*	14	8	11†							29
1		11*	4	5	2			9	10		3		6			7†	12	14				8			30
1			4	5	2		12	9	10†		3		6	14		8		11				7*			31
1			4	5	2*		7	9	10		12		6	14		8		11†				3			32
			4*	5		7	8	9	10†		3		6	14		2		11				12	1		33
		14		5		7	8	9	10				6	4	2*	12		11				3†	1		34
1		14	4	5		7	8†	9	10		3		6	2		12		11*							35
		14	4	5					10		3		6	9*	2	7	8	12				11†		1	36
1	2	3	4	5			8	9					6	10		7		11							37
1			4	5		7	8	9	10		3		6			2		11							38
35	12	19	34	38	13	20	10	37	36	13	28		35	10	14	8	25	23				5	2	1	
	7	9			1		1	1	5	4	1		7	2	13	1	3	1	1	1	1	1			
		2	3	1		2	2	5	13	1			3	7		2		3				1			

43

1990-91

1	Aug	25	(h)	Coventry C	W	2-0	Bruce, Webb	46,715
2		28	(a)	Leeds U	D	0-0		29,172
3	Sep	1	(a)	Sunderland	L	1-2	McClair	26,105
4		4	(a)	Luton T	W	1-0	Robins	12,576
5		8	(h)	QPR	W	3-1	McClair, Robins 2	43,427
6		16	(a)	Liverpool	L	0-4		35,726
7		22	(h)	Southampton	W	3-2	McClair, Blackmore, Hughes	41,228
8		29	(h)	Nottingham F	L	0-1		46,766
9	Oct	20	(h)	Arsenal	L	0-1		47,232
10		27	(a)	Manchester C	D	3-3	Hughes, McClair 2	36,427
11	Nov	3	(h)	Crystal Palace	W	2-0	Webb, Wallace	45,724
12		10	(a)	Derby Co	D	0-0		21,115
13		17	(h)	Sheffield U	W	2-0	Bruce, Hughes	45,903
14		25	(h)	Chelsea	L	2-3	Wallace, Hughes	37,836
15	Dec	1	(a)	Everton	W	1-0	Sharpe	32,400
16		8	(h)	Leeds U	D	1-1	Webb	40,927
17		15	(a)	Coventry C	D	2-2	Hughes, Wallace	17,106
18		22	(a)	Wimbledon	W	3-1	Bruce 2 (2 pens), Hughes	9,744
19		26	(h)	Norwich C	W	3-0	Hughes, McClair 2	39,801
20		29	(h)	Aston Villa	D	1-1	Bruce (pen)	47,485
21	Jan	1	(a)	Tottenham H	W	2-1	Bruce (pen), McClair	29,399
22		12	(h)	Sunderland	W	3-0	Hughes 2, McClair	45,934
23		19	(a)	QPR	D	1-1	Phelan	18,544
24	Feb	3	(h)	Liverpool	D	1-1	Bruce (pen)	43,690
25		26	(a)	Sheffield U	L	1-2	Blackmore (pen)	27,570
26	Mar	2	(h)	Everton	L	0-2		45,656
27		9	(a)	Chelsea	L	2-3	Hughes, McClair	22,818
28		13	(a)	Southampton	D	1-1	Ince	15,701
29		16	(a)	Nottingham F	D	1-1	Blackmore	23,859
30		23	(h)	Luton T	W	4-1	Bruce 2, Robins, McClair	41,752
31		30	(a)	Norwich C	W	3-0	Bruce 2 (1 pen), Ince	18,282
32	Apr	2	(h)	Wimbledon	W	2-1	Bruce, McClair	36,660
33		6	(a)	Aston Villa	D	1-1	Sharpe	33,307
34		16	(h)	Derby Co	W	3-1	Blackmore, McClair, Robson	32,776
35	May	4	(h)	Manchester C	W	1-0	Giggs	45,286
36		6	(a)	Arsenal	L	1-3	Bruce (pen)	40,229
37		11	(a)	Crystal Palace	L	0-3		25,301
38		20	(h)	Tottenham H	D	1-1	Ince	46,791

FINAL LEAGUE POSITION: 6th in Division One

Appearances

Sub. Appearances

Goals

Appearance and scoring grid (Manchester United):

Sealey	Irwin	Donaghy	Bruce	Phelan	Pallister	Webb	Ince	McClair	Hughes	Blackmore	Beardsmore	Robins	Anderson	Sharpe	Martin	Wallace	Robson	Walsh	Ferguson	Giggs	Whitworth	Wratten	Bosnich	Kanchelskis	Match
1	2	3	4	5	6	7	8	9	10	11															1
1	2	3	4	5	6	7	8*	9	10	11	12														2
1	2	3*	4	5	6	7	8	9	10†	11	12	14													3
1	2	14	4	5	6	7	8	9		12	3	11†	10*												4
1	2		4	5	6	7	8	9			3	11	10												5
1	2	14	4	5	6†	7	8*	9	10		3	12	11												6
1	2†	3		5	6	7		9	10	11	12	8*	4	14											7
1	2		4	5	6	7	8	9		12	3	11†	10*												8
1	2†		4	5	6	7	8	9	10		3	12		11*	14										9
1	2		4		6	7	8	9	10	5				11*	3	12									10
1	2		4	5	6	7	8	9			3			11	12	10*									11
1	2†	14	4	5	6	7	8	9	10		3			11*		12									12
1	2*		4	5	6	7	8	9	10		3			11		12									13
1	2		4	5†	6	7	8	9	10		3*		14	12	11										14
1	2		4	5	6	14	8†	9	10		3		7*	12	11										15
1	2*	14	4	5†	6	8		9	10		3		7	11	12										16
1	14		4	5	6	7	8†	9	10	2	3*		11	12											17
1		3	4	5	6	11	8	9	10	2*	12	7													18
1	2	14	4	12	6	5	8	9	10	3	11†	7*													19
1	2		4	12	6	5	8	9	10	3	11	7*													20
1	2†		4	5*	6	7	8	9	10	3	12	11	14												21
1	2		4	12	6	5*	8†	9	10	3	14	11	7												22
1	2	6	4	5		8	9	10	11	7*	12	14	3†												23
1	2		4	5†	6	8*	9	10	3	11	14	12	7												24
	2	5			6	4†	8	9	10		12	3	11	7*	1	14									25
1	2†	5			6	8	9	10	12	7	3*	11		4	14										26
1		4	5	6		8	9	10	2*	11	3	12	7												27
1		4	5	6		8	9		7*	12	11	3	10		14	2†									28
1	2	12	4	5	6	8	10	9	3*	11	7														29
1	2		4	5	6	9	10	3	12	11	8*	7													30
1	2*		4	5	6	9	8	12	10	3	14	11†	7												31
	2	3	4†	5	6	7	8	9	10	12	11*	1				14									32
1	2	3	4	5*	6	8	9	10	12	11	7														33
	2	3	4	6	5*	8	12	10	9	11	7	1													34
	2	12	4	5	6	8	9	10	3	7	1	11*													35
		6	4	2		5	8	9	10*	3	12	11	7†	1	14										36
	2	3	4	6*	5	8		12	9†	11	1	10	14	7											37
	2†	14	4	5	6	8	9	10	3	12	11*	7	1												38
31	33	17	31	30	36	31	31	34	29	35	5	7	1	20	7	13	15	5	2	1	1		2	1	
	1		8		3		1		2	2		7	12	3	7	6	2		3	1	2				
			13	1		3	3	13	10	4		4		2		3	1		1						

45

1991-92

#	Month	Date		Opponent	Result	Score	Scorers	Attendance
1	Aug	17	(h)	Notts Co	W	2-0	Hughes, Robson	46,278
2		21	(a)	Aston Villa	W	1-0	Bruce (pen)	39,995
3		24	(a)	Everton	D	0-0		36,085
4		28	(h)	Oldham A	W	1-0	McClair	42,078
5		31	(h)	Leeds U	D	1-1	Robson	43,778
6	Sep	3	(a)	Wimbledon	W	2-1	Blackmore, Pallister	13,824
7		7	(h)	Norwich C	W	3-0	Irwin, McClair, Giggs	44,946
8		14	(a)	Southampton	W	1-0	Hughes	19,264
9		21	(h)	Luton T	W	5-0	Ince, Bruce (pen), McClair 2, Hughes	46,491
10		28	(a)	Tottenham H	W	2-1	Hughes, Robson	35,087
11	Oct	6	(h)	Liverpool	D	0-0		44,997
12		19	(h)	Arsenal	D	1-1	Bruce	46,594
13		26	(a)	Sheffield W	L	2-3	McClair 2	38,260
14	Nov	2	(h)	Sheffield U	W	2-0	Beesley (og), Kanchelskis	42,942
15		16	(a)	Manchester C	D	0-0		38,180
16		23	(h)	West Ham U	W	2-1	Giggs, Robson	47,185
17		30	(a)	Crystal Palace	W	3-1	Webb, McClair, Kanchelskis	29,017
18	Dec	7	(h)	Coventry C	W	4-0	Bruce, Webb, McClair, Hughes	42,549
19		15	(a)	Chelsea	W	3-1	Irwin, McClair, Bruce (pen)	23,120
20		26	(a)	Oldham A	W	6-3	Irwin 2, Kanchelskis, McClair 2, Giggs	18,947
21		29	(a)	Leeds U	D	1-1	Webb	32,638
22	Jan	1	(h)	QPR	L	1-4	McClair	38,554
23		11	(h)	Everton	W	1-0	Kanchelskis	46,619
24		18	(a)	Notts Co	D	1-1	Blackmore (pen)	21,055
25		22	(h)	Aston Villa	W	1-0	Hughes	45,022
26	Feb	1	(a)	Arsenal	D	1-1	McClair	41,703
27		8	(h)	Sheffield W	D	1-1	McClair	47,074
28		22	(h)	Crystal Palace	W	2-0	Hughes 2	46,347
29		26	(h)	Chelsea	D	1-1	Hughes	44,872
30		29	(a)	Coventry C	D	0-0		23,967
31	Mar	14	(a)	Sheffield U	W	2-1	McClair, Blackmore	30,183
32		18	(a)	Nottingham F	L	0-1		28,062
33		21	(h)	Wimbledon	D	0-0		45,428
34		28	(a)	QPR	D	0-0		22,603
35		31	(a)	Norwich C	W	3-1	Ince 2, McClair	17,489
36	Apr	7	(h)	Manchester C	D	1-1	Giggs	46,781
37		16	(h)	Southampton	W	1-0	Kanchelskis	43,972
38		18	(a)	Luton T	D	1-1	Sharpe	13,410
39		20	(h)	Nottingham F	L	1-2	McClair	47,576
40		22	(a)	West Ham U	L	0-1		24,197
41		26	(a)	Liverpool	L	0-2		38,669
42	May	2	(h)	Tottenham H	W	3-1	McClair, Hughes 2	44,595

FINAL LEAGUE POSITION: 2nd in Division One

Appearances

Sub. Appearances

Goals

Schmeichel	Irwin	Blackmore	Bruce	Ferguson	Parker	Robson	Ince	McClair	Hughes	Kanchelskis	Pallister	Giggs	Donaghy	Webb	Phelan	Martin	Robins	Sharpe	Walsh	
1	2	3	4	5†	6	7	8*	9	10	11	12	14								1
1	2	3	4		6	7	8	9	10	11			5							2
1	2†	3*	4		6	7	8	9	10		14	11	5	12						3
1	3	12	4	14	2	7	8*	9	10		6	11	5†							4
1	3	11	4†		2	7	8*	9	10		6	12	5	14						5
1	12	11	4		2	7		9	10		6		3	8	5*					6
1	3	12	4		2	7		9	10	8*	6	11	5†	14						7
1	3		4			7	12	9	10	8*	6	11		5	2					8
1	3	9*	4			7	8	12	10		6	11		5	2					9
1	3	12	4			7	8	9	10	5*	6	11			2					10
1	3	5	4			7	8†	9	10	12	6	11	14		2*					11
1	3	2	4			7	8	9	10	12	6	11	5*							12
1	3	10	4*		2	7		9		8	6	11		5				12		13
1		3	4		2	12	8	9		7*	14	11†	6	5				10		14
1	3	8	4		2	7	12	9	10		6	11	5*							15
1	3	12	4		2*	7		9	10	8	6	11	5							16
1	3*	12	4		2	7		9	10	8	6	11	5							17
1	3	12	4		2*		8	9	10	7	6	11	5							18
1	3	12	4		2		8	9	10	7	6	11*	5							19
1	3*	12	4		2	7†	8	9	10	11	6	14	5							20
1		3*	4		2		8	9	10	7†	6	11	14	5				12		21
1		3	4		2		8	9	10		6	12	5	7*				11		22
1		3*	4		2		8	9	10	7	6	11	12	5						23
1	3	12	4*		2		8	9	10	7	6	11†		5			14			24
1	3		4			7	8	9	10	11	6		2	5						25
1	3				4	7	8*	9	10	11	6	12	2	5						26
1	3					7	8	9	10	11	6		2*	5	5†	14		12		27
1	3				14	7	8	9	10	11*	6		4	2	5†			12		28
	3	12			14	7†	8	9	10	11*	6		4	2	5				1	29
	3	12			2		8	9	10	7*	6	11	4	5					1	30
1	3	12	4*		2	7	8	9		11	6		2	5				10		31
1	3	2	4				8	9	10*	12	6	14		5†	7			11		32
1	3	2	4				8	9	10	7	6	11		5*				12		33
1	3		4			7		9	10	8*	6	11	2	5				12		34
1	3	12	4			7*	8	9	10		6		5	2				11		35
1	3	5*	4				8	9	10	12	6		7	2				11		36
1	3		4		2		8*	9	10	7	6	11	12	5						37
1	3	14	4		2†			9	10*	12	6	7		8	5			11		38
1	3	2	4					9	12	7	6	10	14	8*	5			11†		39
1	2	8*	4	14				9	10	12	6	7	3†	5				11		40
1	2		4			7	8	9	10	5	6*	11	3					12		41
1	3		4		2		8*	9	10	7	6	11		5				12		42
40	37	19	37	2	24	26	31	41	38	28	37	32	16	29	14		1	8	2	
	1	14		2	2	1	2	1	1	6	3	6	4	2	4	1	1	6		
	4	3	5			4	3	18	11	5	1	4		3				1		

1992-93

#		Date		Opponent		Result	Score	Scorers	Attendance
1	Aug	15	(a)	Sheffield U	L	1-2	Hughes		28,070
2		19	(h)	Everton	L	0-3			31,901
3		22	(h)	Ipswich T	D	1-1	Irwin		31,704
4		24	(a)	Southampton	W	1-0	Dublin		15,623
5		29	(a)	Nottingham F	W	2-0	Hughes, Giggs		19,694
6	Sep	2	(h)	Crystal Palace	W	1-0	Hughes		29,736
7		6	(h)	Leeds U	W	2-0	Kanchelskis, Bruce		31,296
8		12	(a)	Everton	W	2-0	McClair, Bruce (pen)		30,002
9		19	(a)	Tottenham H	D	1-1	Giggs		33,296
10		26	(h)	QPR	D	0-0			33,287
11	Oct	3	(a)	Middlesbrough	D	1-1	Bruce (pen)		24,172
12		18	(h)	Liverpool	D	2-2	Hughes 2		33,243
13		24	(a)	Blackburn R	D	0-0			20,305
14		31	(h)	Wimbledon	L	0-1			32,622
15	Nov	7	(a)	Aston Villa	L	0-1			39,063
16		21	(h)	Oldham A	W	3-0	McClair, Hughes		33,497
17		28	(a)	Arsenal	W	1-0	Hughes		29,739
18	Dec	6	(h)	Manchester C	W	2-1	Ince, Hughes		35,408
19		12	(h)	Norwich C	W	1-0	Hughes		34,500
20		19	(a)	Chelsea	D	1-1	Cantona		34,464
21		26	(a)	Sheffield W	D	3-3	McClair 2, Cantona		37,708
22		28	(h)	Coventry C	W	5-0	Giggs, Hughes, Cantona (pen), Sharpe, Irwin		36,025
23	Jan	9	(h)	Tottenham H	W	4-1	Cantona, Irwin, McClair, Parker		35,648
24		18	(a)	QPR	W	3-1	Ince, Giggs, Kanchelskis		21,177
25		27	(h)	Nottingham F	W	2-0	Ince, Hughes		36,085
26		30	(a)	Ipswich T	L	1-2	McClair		22,068
27	Feb	6	(h)	Sheffield U	W	2-1	McClair, Cantona		36,156
28		8	(a)	Leeds U	D	0-0			34,166
29		20	(h)	Southampton	W	2-1	Giggs 2		36,257
30		27	(h)	Middlesbrough	W	3-0	Giggs, Irwin, Cantona		36,251
31	Mar	6	(a)	Liverpool	W	2-1	Hughes, McClair		44,374
32		9	(a)	Oldham A	L	0-1			17,106
33		14	(h)	Aston Villa	D	1-1	Hughes		36,163
34		20	(a)	Manchester C	D	1-1	Cantona		37,136
35		24	(h)	Arsenal	D	0-0			37,301
36	Apr	5	(a)	Norwich C	W	3-1	Giggs, Kanchelskis, Cantona		20,582
37		10	(h)	Sheffield W	W	2-1	Bruce 2		40,102
38		12	(a)	Coventry C	W	1-0	Irwin		24,429
39		17	(h)	Chelsea	W	3-0	Hughes, Clarke (og), Cantona		40,139
40		21	(a)	Crystal Palace	W	2-0	Hughes, Ince		30,115
41	May	3	(h)	Blackburn R	W	3-1	Giggs, Ince, Pallister		40,447
42		9	(a)	Wimbledon	W	2-1	Ince, Robson		30,115

FINAL LEAGUE POSITION: 1st in Premier League

Appearances

Sub. Appearances

Goals

Schmeichel	Irwin	Blackmore	Bruce	Ferguson	Pallister	Kanchelskis	Ince	McClair	Hughes	Giggs	Phelan	Dublin	Webb	Wallace	Robson	Parker	Sharpe	Butt	Cantona	No
1	2	3	4	5	6	7†	8*	9	10	11	12	14								1
1	2	3	4	5	6	7	8*	9	10	11†	12	14								2
1	2	3†	4	5	6	7*		9	10	11	8	12	14							3
1	3		4	5	6		8	9	10	11	2	7								4
1	3	14	4	5	6	12	8	9	10*	11	2†	7								5
1	3	2	4	5	6	12	8	9	10	11		7*								6
1	3	2	4	5	6	7	8	9	10	11										7
1	2	3	4	5	6	7	8	9	10	11										8
1	2	3	4	5	6	7*	8	9	10	11			12							9
1	2	3	4	5	6	7*	8	9	10	11			12							10
1	2	7	4	5	6	12	8	9	10†	11	3*			14						11
1	3	12	4	5	6	7*	8	9	10	11						2				12
1	3	7	4	5*	6	12	8	9	10	11						2				13
1		3	4	5	6	7*	8	9	10	11					12	2				14
1		3	4	5*	6		8	12	10	11					7	2	9			15
1	3*		4		6		8†	9	10	11	12				7	2	5	14		16
1	3		4		6		8	9	10	11					7	2	5			17
1	3		4		6		8	9	10	11*					7	2	5	12		18
1	3		4		6		8	9	10	11						2	5		7	19
1	3		4		6	12	8	9	10		5*					2	11		7	20
1	3		4		6	12	8	9	10	11*						2	5		7	21
1	3		4†		6	12	8	9	10	11*	14					2	5		7	22
1	3		4		6	12	8†	9	10	11*	14					2	5		7	23
1	3		4		6	7	8	9	10*	11	12					2	5			24
1	3		4		6		8	9	10	11						2	5		7	25
1	3		4		6	12	8	9	10	11						2	5*		7	26
1	3		4		6	12	8	9	10	11*						2	5		7	27
1	3		4		6	12	8	9	10	11*						2	5		7	28
1	3		4		6		8	9	10	11						2	5		7	29
1	3		4		6		8	9	10	11						2	5		7	30
1	3		4		6	7	8	9	10	11						2	5			31
1	3		4		6	7*	8	9	10	11	12					2	5			32
1	3		4		6		8	9	10	11						2	5		7	33
1	3		4		6		8	9	10	11						2	5		7	34
1	3		4		6		8	9	10*	11					12	2	5		7	35
1	3		4		6	10*	8	9		11					12	2	5		7	36
1	3		4		6		8	9	10	11					12	2*	5		7	37
1	3		4		6		8	9	10	11					12	2	5		7*	38
1	3		4		6	14	8	9*	10	11†					12	2	5		7	39
1	3		4		6	5*	8	9	10	11					12	2			7	40
1	3		4		6	14	8	9†	10	11					12	2	5*		7	41
1	3*		4		6		8	9	10	12					7	2	5		11	42
42	40	12	42	15	42	14	41	41	41	40	5	3			5	31	27		21	
	2					13		1		1	6	4	1	2	9		1		1	
	5		5		1	3	6	9	15	9		1			1		1		9	

1993-94

1	Aug	15	(a)	Norwich C	W	2-0	Robson, Giggs	19,705
2		18	(h)	Sheffield U	W	3-0	Keane 2, Hughes	41,949
3		21	(h)	Newcastle U	D	1-1	Giggs	41,829
4		23	(a)	Aston Villa	W	2-1	Sharpe 2	39,624
5		28	(a)	Southampton	W	3-1	Irwin, Sharpe, Cantona	16,189
6	Sep	1	(h)	West Ham U	W	3-0	Bruce, Sharpe, Cantona	44,613
7		11	(a)	Chelsea	L	0-1		37,064
8		19	(h)	Arsenal	W	1-0	Cantona	44,009
9		25	(h)	Swindon T	W	4-2	Cantona, Hughes 2, Kanchelskis	44,583
10	Oct	2	(a)	Sheffield W	W	3-2	Hughes 2, Giggs	34,548
11		16	(h)	Tottenham H	W	2-1	Sharpe, Keane	44,655
12		23	(a)	Everton	W	1-0	Sharpe	35,430
13		30	(h)	Q.P.R.	W	2-1	Cantona, Hughes	44,663
14	Nov	7	(a)	Manchester C	W	3-2	Cantona 2, Keane	35,155
15		20	(h)	Wimbledon	W	3-1	Pallister, Hughes, Kanchelskis	44,748
16		24	(h)	Ipswich T	D	0-0		43,300
17		27	(a)	Coventry C	W	1-0	Cantona	17,020
18	Dec	4	(h)	Norwich C	D	2-2	McClair, Giggs	44,694
19		7	(a)	Sheffield U	W	3-0	Sharpe, Cantona, Hughes	26,746
20		11	(a)	Newcastle U	D	1-1	Ince	36,388
21		19	(h)	Aston Villa	W	3-1	Cantona 2, Ince	44,499
22		26	(h)	Blackburn R	D	1-1	Ince	44,511
23		29	(a)	Oldham Ath	W	5-2	Bruce, Cantona, Kanchelskis, Giggs 2	16,708
24	Jan	1	(h)	Leeds U	D	0-0		44,724
25		4	(a)	Liverpool	D	3-3	Irwin, Bruce, Giggs	42,795
26		15	(a)	Tottenham H	W	1-0	Hughes	31,343
27		22	(h)	Everton	W	1-0	Giggs	44,750
28	Feb	5	(a)	Q.P.R.	W	3-2	Kanchelskis, Cantona, Giggs	21,267
29		26	(a)	West Ham U	D	2-2	Ince, Hughes	28,832
30	Mar	5	(h)	Chelsea	L	0-1		44,745
31		14	(h)	Sheffield W	W	5-0	Cantona 2, Ince, Hughes, Giggs	43,669
32		19	(a)	Swindon T	D	2-2	Keane, Ince	18,102
33		22	(a)	Arsenal	D	2-2	Sharpe 2	36,203
34		30	(h)	Liverpool	W	1-0	Ince	44,751
35	Apr	2	(a)	Blackburn R	L	0-2		20,886
36		4	(h)	Oldham Ath	W	3-2	Ince, Giggs, Dublin	44,686
37		16	(a)	Wimbledon	L	0-1		28,553
38		23	(h)	Manchester C	W	2-0	Cantona 2	44,333
39		27	(a)	Leeds U	W	2-0	Kanchelskis, Giggs	41,125
40	May	1	(a)	Ipswich T	W	2-1	Cantona, Giggs	22,559
41		4	(h)	Southampton	W	2-0	Kanchelskis, Hughes	44,705
42		8	(h)	Coventry City	D	0-0		44,717

FINAL LEAGUE POSITION: 1st in F.A. Premiership

Appearances

Sub. Appearances

Goals

50

Schmeichel	Parker	Irwin	Bruce	Kanchelskis	Pallister	Robson	Ince	Keane	Hughes	Giggs	McClair	Sharpe	Cantona	Butt	Martin	Phelan	Ferguson	Thornley	Dublin	Walsh	Neville G.	McKee	No.
1	2	3	4	5	6	7	8	9	10	11													1
1	2	3	4	5	6	7	8	9	10	11	12												2
1	2	3	4	5	6	7	8	9	10	11	14	12											3
1	2	3	4	7	6		8	9	10	11		5											4
1	2	3	4	14	6		8	9	10	11	12	5	7										5
1	2	3	4	10	6	14	8	9		11	12	5	7										6
1	2	3	4		6	10	8	9		11	12	5	7										7
1	2	3	4		6		8	9	10	11	12	5	7										8
1	2	3	4	11	6		8	9	10	14	12	5	7										9
1	2	3	4	12	6		8	9	10	11		5	7										10
1	2	3	4		6	8		9	10	11	12	5	7	14									11
1		3	4		6		8	11	10		9	5	7		2								12
1	2	3	4				8	9	10	11		5	7			6							13
1	2	3	4	11	6		8	9	10	14		5	7										14
1	2	3	4	11	6	9	8		10			5	7				12						15
1	2	3	4	11	6	9	8		10	14		5	7				12						16
1	2	3	4		6		8		10	11		5	7				9						17
1	2	3	4	5	6		8		10	11	9	14	7										18
1	2	3	4		6		8	12	10	11	9	5	7										19
1	2	3	4	12	6		8	14	10	11	9	5	7										20
1	2	3	4	11	6		8	9	10	12		5	7										21
1	2	3	4		6		8	9	10	11	12	5	7			14							22
1	2	3	4	10	6	14	8	9		11	12	5	7										23
1	2	3	4	10	6	5	8			11	9		7										24
1	2	3	4	10	6		8	5		11	9		7										25
1	2	3	4	5	6		8	9	10	11	12		7										26
1	2	3	4	5	6		8	9	10	11			7										27
1	2	3	4	5	6		8	9	10	11			7										28
1	2	3	4	5	6		8	11	10		9		7					12	14				29
1	2	3	4	5	6	12	8	7	10	11	9								14				30
1	2	3	4	5	6	14	8	9	10	11	12		7										31
1	2	3	4		6		8	5	10	11	9		7										32
1	2	3	4		6		8	9	10	11	12	5	7										33
1	2	3	4	11	6	14	8	9	10	12		5	7										34
1	2	3	4	7	6		8	9	10	11	12	5											35
1		3	4	7	6		8	2	10	11	9	5							12				36
1	2	3	4	5	6	7	8		10	11	9	12							14				37
1	2	3	4	11	6		8	9	10	12		5	7										38
1	2	3	4	5	6		8	9	10	11			7										39
1	2	3	4	5	6		8	9	10	11		14	7						12				40
	2	3		4	6		8	9	10	11		5	7							1			41
12		3	4		6	10		14			9	5	7						11	1	2	8	42
40	39	42	41	28	41	10	39	34	36	32	12	26	34	-	1	1	1	-	1	2	1	1	
	1			3		5		3		6	14	4		1		1	2	1	4	1			
		2	3	6	1	1	8	5	12	13	1	9	18			1							

51

F.A. CUP COMPETITION
1984/85 SEASON
3rd Round
Jan 5 vs Bournemouth (h) 3-0
Att: 32,080   Strachan, McQueen, Stapleton
4th Round
Jan 26 vs Coventry City (h) 2-1
Att: 38,039   Hughes, McGrath
5th Round
Feb 15 vs Blackburn Rovers (a) 2-0
Att: 22,692   Strachan, McGrath
6th Round
Mar 9 vs West Ham United (h) 4-2
Att: 46,769   Hughes, Whiteside 3 (1 pen)
Semi-Final
Apr 13 vs Liverpool 2-2
Att: 51,690 (at Villa Park)   Robson, Stapleton
Semi-Final Replay
Apr 17 vs Liverpool 2-1
Att: 45,775 (at Maine Road)   Robson, Hughes
FINAL
May 18 vs Everton 1-0 (aet) (90 mins 0-0)
Att: 100,000 (at Wembley)   Whiteside

1985/86 SEASON
3rd Round
Jan 9 vs Rochdale (h) 2-0
Att: 38,500   Stapleton, Hughes
4th Round
Jan 25 vs Sunderland (a) 0-0
Att: 35,484
Replay
Jan 29 vs Sunderland (h) 3-0
Att: 43,402   Whiteside, Olsen 2 (1 pen)
5th Round
Mar 5 vs West Ham United (a) 1-1
Att: 26,441   Stapleton
Replay
Mar 9 vs West Ham United (h) 0-2
Att: 30,441

1986/87 SEASON
3rd Round
Jan 10 vs Manchester City (h) 1-0
Att: 54,294   Whiteside
4th Round
Jan 31 vs Coventry City (h) 0-1
Att: 49,082

1987/88 SEASON
3rd Round
Jan 10 vs Ipswich Town (a) 2-1
Att: 23,012   D'Avray (og), Anderson
4th Round
Jan 30 vs Chelsea (h) 2-0
Att: 50,716   Whiteside, McClair

5th Round
Feb 20 vs Arsenal (a) 1-2
Att: 32,222   McClair

1988/89 SEASON
3rd Round
Jan 7 vs Queens Park Rangers (h) 0-0
Att: 36,222
Replay
Jan 11 vs Queens Park Rangers (a) 2-2 (aet)
Att: 22,236   Gill, Graham
2nd Replay
Jan 23 vs Queens Park Rangers (h) 3-0
Att: 46,257   McClair 2 (1 pen), Robson
4th Round
Jan 28 vs Oxford United (h) 4-0
Att: 47,754   Hughes, Bruce, Phillips J (og), Robson
5th Round
Feb 18 vs Bournemouth (a) 1-1
Att: 12,500   Hughes
Replay
Feb 22 vs Bournemouth (h) 1-0
Att: 52,422   McClair
6th Round
Mar 18 vs Nottingham Forest (h) 0-1
Att: 55,052

1989/90 SEASON
3rd Round
Jan 7 vs Nottingham Forest (a) 1-0
Att: 23,072   Robins
4th Round
Jan 28 vs Hereford United (a) 1-0
Att: 13,777   Blackmore
5th Round
Feb 18 vs Newcastle United (a) 3-2
Att: 31,748   Robins, Wallace, McClair
6th Round
Mar 11 vs Sheffield United (a) 1-0
Att: 34,344   McClair
Semi-Final
Apr 8 vs Oldham Athletic 3-3 (aet)
Att: 44,026 (at Maine Road)   Robson, Webb, Wallace
Replay
Apr 11 vs Oldham Athletic 2-1 (aet)
Att: 35,005 (at Maine Road)   McClair, Robins
FINAL
May 12 vs Crystal Palace 3-3 (aet)
Att: 80,000 (at Wembley)   Robson, Hughes 2
REPLAY
May 17 vs Crystal Palace 1-0
Att: 80,000 (at Wembley)   Martin

1990/91 SEASON
3rd Round
Jan 7 vs Queens Park Rangers (h) 2-1
Att: 35,065   Hughes, McClair

4th Round
Jan 26 vs Bolton Wanderers (h) 1-0
Att: 43,293   Hughes

5th Round
Feb 18 vs Norwich City (a) 1-2
Att: 23,058   McClair

1991/92 SEASON
3rd Round
Jan 15 vs Leeds United (a) 1-0
Att: 31,819   Hughes

4th Round
Jan 27 vs Southampton (a) 0-0
Att: 19,506

Replay
Feb 5 vs Southampton (h) 2-2 (aet)
Att: 33,414   Kanchelskis, McClair
Southampton won 4-2 on penalties

1992/93 SEASON
3rd Round
Jan 5 vs Bury (h) 2-0
Att: 30,668   Phelan, Gillespie

4th Round
Jan 23 vs Brighton & Hove Albion (h) 1-0
Att: 33,610   Giggs

5th Round
Jan 14 vs Sheffield United (a) 1-2
Att: 27,150   Giggs

1993/94 SEASON
3rd Round
Jan 9 vs Sheffield United (a) 1-0
Att: 22,019   Hughes

4th Round
Jan 30 vs Norwich City (a) 2-0
Att: 21,060   Keane, Cantona

5th Round
Feb 20 vs Wimbledon (a) 3-0
Att: 27,511   Irwin, Cantona, Ince

6th Round
Mar 12 vs Charlton Athletic (h) 3-1
Att: 44,347   Kanchelskis 2, Hughes

Semi-Final
Apr 10 vs Oldham Athletic 1-1
Att: 56,399 (at Wembley)   Hughes

Replay
Apr 13 vs Oldham Athletic 4-1
Att: 32,311 (at Maine Road)   Irwin, Kanchelskis, Robson, Giggs

FINAL
May 14 vs Chelsea 4-0
Att: 79,634 (at Wembley)   Cantona 2 (2 pens), Hughes, McClair

LEAGUE CUP COMPETITION
1984/85 SEASON
2nd Round (1st leg)
Sep 26 vs Burnley (h) 4-0
Att: 28,283   Robson, Hughes 3

2nd Round (2nd leg)
Oct 9 vs Burnley (a) 3-0 (aggregate 7-0)
Att: 12,684   Brazil 2, Olsen

3rd Round
Oct 30 vs Everton (h) 1-2
Att: 50,918   Brazil

1985/86 SEASON
2nd Round (1st leg)
Sep 24 vs Crystal Palace (a) 1-0
Att: 21,506   Barnes

2nd Round (2nd leg)
Oct 7 vs Crystal Palace (h) 1-0 (aggregate 2-0)
Att: 26,118   Whiteside

3rd Round
Oct 29 vs West Ham United (h) 1-0
Att: 32,057   Whiteside

4th Round
Nov 26 vs Liverpool (a) 1-2
Att: 41,291   McGrath

1986/87 SEASON
2nd Round (1st leg)
Sep 24 vs Port Vale (h) 2-0
Att: 18,906   Stapleton, Whiteside

2nd Round (2nd leg)
Oct 7 vs Port vale (a) 5-2 (aggregate 7-2)
Att: 10,486   Stapleton, Barnes, Moses 2, Davenport (pen)

3rd Round
Oct 29 vs Southampton (h) 0-0
Att: 23,639

Replay
Nov 4 vs Southampton (a) 1-4
Att: 17,915   Davenport

1987/88 SEASON
2nd Round (1st leg)
Sep 23 vs Hull City (h) 5-0
Att: 25,041   McGrath, Davenport, Whiteside, Strachan, McClair

2nd Round (2nd leg)
Oct 7 vs Hull City (a) 1-0 (aggregate 6-0)
Att: 13,586   McClair

3rd Round
Oct 28 vs Crystal Palace (h) 2-1
Att: 27,283   McClair 2 (1 pen)

4th Round
Nov 18 vs Bury (a) (at Old Trafford) 2-1
Att: 33,519   Whiteside, McClair

Quarter-Final
Jan 20 vs Oxford United (a) 0-2
Att: 12,658

1988/89 SEASON
2nd Round (1st leg)
Sep 28 vs Rotherham United (a) 1-0
Att: 12,592   Davenport

2nd Round (2nd leg)
Oct 12 vs Rotherham United (h) 5-0 (agg. 6-0)
Att: 20,597   McClair 3, Robson, Bruce

3rd Round
Nov 2 vs Wimbledon (a) 1-2
Att: 10,864   Robson

1989/90 SEASON
2nd Round (1st leg)
Sep 20 vs Portsmouth (a) 3-2
Att: 18,072   Ince 2, Wallace

2nd Round (2nd leg)
Oct 3 vs Portsmouth (h) 0-0 (aggregate 3-2)
Att: 26,698

3rd Round
Oct 25 vs Tottenham Hotspur (h) 0-3
Att: 45,759

1990/91 SEASON
2nd Round (1st leg)
Sep 26 vs Halifax Town (a) 3-1
Att: 7,500   Blackmore, McClair, Webb

2nd Round (2nd leg)
Oct 10 vs Halifax Town (h) 2-1 (aggregate 5-2)
Att: 22,295   Bruce (pen), Anderson

3rd Round
Oct 31 vs Liverpool (h) 3-1
Att: 42,033   Bruce (pen), Hughes, Sharpe

4th Round
Nov 28 vs Arsenal (a) 6-2
Att: 40,884   Blackmore, Hughes, Sharpe 3, Wallace

Quarter-Final
Jan 16 vs Southampton (a) 1-1
Att: 21,011   Hughes

Replay
Jan 23 vs Southampton (h) 3-2
Att: 41,093   Hughes 3

Semi-Final (1st leg)
Feb 10 vs Leeds United (h) 2-1
Att: 34,050   Sharpe, McClair

Semi-Final (2nd leg)
Feb 24 vs Leeds United (a) 1-0 (aggregate 3-1)
Att: 32,014   Sharpe

FINAL
Apr 21 vs Sheffield Wednesday 0-1
Att: 80,000 (at Wembley)

1991/92 SEASON
2nd Round (1st leg)
Sep 25 vs Cambridge United (h) 3-0
Att: 30,934   Giggs, McClair, Bruce

2nd Round (2nd leg)
Oct 9 vs Cambridge United (a) 1-1 (agg. 4-1)
Att: 9,248   McClair

3rd Round
Oct 30 vs Portsmouth (h) 3-1
Att: 29,543   Robins 2, Robson

4th Round
Dec 4 vs Oldham Athletic (h) 2-0
Att: 38,550   McClair, Kanchelskis

Quarter-Final
Jan 8 vs Leeds United (a) 3-1
Att: 28,886   Blackmore, Kanchelskis, Giggs

Semi-Final (1st leg)
Mar 4 vs Middlesbrough (a) 0-0
Att: 25,572

Semi-Final (2nd leg)
Mar 11 vs Middlesbrough (h) 2-1 (aggregate 2-1)
Att: 45,875   Sharpe, Giggs

FINAL
Apr 12 vs Nottingham Forest 1-0
Att: 76,810   McClair

1992/93 SEASON
2nd Round (1st leg)
Sep 23 vs Brighton & Hove Albion (a) 1-1
Att: 16,649   Wallace

2nd Round (2nd leg)
Oct 7 vs Brighton & Hove Alb. (h) 1-0 (agg. 2-1)
Att: 25,405   Hughes

3rd Round
Oct 28 vs Aston Villa (a) 0-1
Att: 35,964

1993/94 SEASON
2nd Round (1st leg)
Sep 22 vs Stoke City (a) 1-2
Att: 23,327   Dublin

2nd Round (2nd leg)
Oct 6 vs Stoke City (h) 2-0 (aggregate 3-2)
Att: 41,387   Sharpe, McClair

3rd Round
Oct 27 vs Leicester City (h) 5-1
Att: 41,344   Bruce 2, Sharpe, McClair, Hughes

4th Round
Nov 30 vs Everton (a) 2-0
Att: 34,052   Hughes, Giggs

Quarter-Final
Jan 12 vs Portsmouth (h) 2-2
Att: 43,794   Cantona, Giggs

Replay
Jan 26 vs Portsmouth (a) 1-0
Att: 24,950   McClair

Semi-Final (1st leg)
Feb 13 vs Sheffield Wednesday (h) 1-0
Att: 43,294   Giggs
Semi-Final (2nd leg)
Mar 2 vs Sheffield Wednesday (a) 4-1 (agg. 5-1)
Att: 34,878   Kanchelskis, McClair, Hughes 2
FINAL
Mar 27 vs Aston Villa 1-3
Att: 77,231 (at Wembley)   Hughes

EUROPEAN CHAMPIONS CUP

1993/94 SEASON
1st Round (1st leg)
Sep 15 vs Honved (a) 3-2
Att: 9,000   Cantona, Keane 2

1st Round (2nd leg)
Sep 29 vs Honved (h) 2-1 (aggregate 5-3)
Att: 35,781   Bruce 2

2nd Round (1st leg)
Oct 20 vs Galatasaray (h) 3-3
Att: 39,346   Robson, Hakan (og), Cantona

2nd Round (2nd leg)
Nov 3 vs Galatasaray (a) 0-0 (aggregate 3-3)
Att: 40,000   Galatasaray win on away goals

EUROPEAN CUP-WINNERS CUP

1990/91 SEASON
1st Round (1st leg)
Sep 19 vs Pecsi Munkas (h) 2-0
Att: 26,411   Blackmore, Webb

1st Round (2nd leg)
Oct 3 vs Pecsi Munkas (a) 1-0 (aggregate 3-0)
Att: 15,000   McClair

2nd Round (1st leg)
Oct 23 vs Wrexham (h) 3-0
Att: 29,405   McClair, Bruce (pen), Pallister

2nd Round (2nd leg)
Nov 7 vs Wrexham (a) 2-0 (aggregate 5-0)
Att: 13,327   Robins, Bruce

Quarter-Final (1st leg)
Mar 6 vs Montpellier (h) 1-1
Att: 41,942   McClair

Quarter-Final (2nd leg)
Mar 19 vs Montpellier (a) 2-0 (aggregate 3-1)
Att: 20,500   Blackmore, Bruce (pen)

Semi-Final (1st leg)
Apr 10 vs Legia Warsaw (a) 3-1
Att: 17,500   McClair, Hughes, Bruce

Semi-Final (2nd leg)
Apr 24 vs Legia Warsaw (h) 1-1 (aggregate 4-2)
Att: 44,269   Sharpe

FINAL
May 15 vs Barcelona 2-1
Att: 45,000 (in Rotterdam)   Hughes 2

1991/92 SEASON
1st Round (1st leg)
Sep 18 vs Athinaikos (a) 0-0
Att: 9,500

1st Round (2nd leg)
Oct 2 vs Athinaikos (h) 2-0 (aet) (aggregate 2-0)
Att: 35,023   Hughes, McClair

2nd Round (1st leg)
Oct 23 vs Atletico Madrid (a) 0-3
Att: 52,000

2nd Round (2nd leg)
Nov 6 vs Atletico Madrid (h) 1-1 (aggregate 1-4)
Att: 39,654   Hughes

UEFA CUP

1984/85 SEASON
1st Round (1st leg)
Sep 19 vs Raba Gyor (h) 3-0
Att: 32,537   Robson, Muhren, Hughes

1st Round (2nd leg)
Oct 3 vs Raba Gyor (a) 2-2 (aggregate 5-2)
Att: 28,000   Brazil, Muhren (pen)

2nd Round (1st leg)
Oct 24 vs PSV Eindhoven (a) 0-0
Att: 26,500

2nd Round (2nd leg)
Nov 7 vs PSV Eindhoven (h) 1-0 (aggregate 1-0)
Att: 39,281   Strachan (pen)

3rd Round (1st leg)
Nov 28 vs Dundee United (h) 2-2
Att: 48,278   Strachan (pen), Robson

3rd Round (2nd leg)
Dec 12 vs Dundee United (a) 3-2 (aggregate 5-4)
Att: 22,500   Hughes, McGinnis (og), Muhren

Quarter-Final (1st leg)
Mar 6 vs Videoton (h) 1-0
Att: 35,432   Stapleton

Quarter-Final (2nd leg)
Mar 20 vs Videoton (a) 0-1 (aet) (aggregate 1-1)
Att: 25,000   Videoton won 5-4 on penalties

1984-85 SEASON

FIRST DIVISION

Everton	42	28	6	8	88	43	90
Liverpool	42	22	11	9	78	35	77
Tottenham Hotspur	42	23	8	11	78	51	77
Manchester United	**42**	**22**	**10**	**10**	**77**	**47**	**76**
Southampton	42	19	11	12	56	47	68
Chelsea	42	18	12	12	63	48	66
Arsenal	42	19	9	14	61	49	66
Sheffield Wednesday	42	17	14	11	58	45	65
Nottingham Forest	42	19	7	16	56	48	64
Aston Villa	42	15	11	16	60	60	56
Watford	42	14	13	15	81	71	55
West Brom	42	16	7	19	58	62	55
Luton Town	42	15	9	18	57	61	54
Newcastle United	42	13	13	16	55	70	52
Leicester City	42	15	6	21	65	73	51
West Ham United	42	13	12	17	51	68	51
Ipswich Town	42	13	11	18	46	57	50
Coventry City	42	15	5	22	47	64	50
QPR	42	13	11	18	53	72	50
Norwich City	42	13	10	19	46	64	49
Sunderland	42	10	10	22	40	62	40
Stoke City	42	3	8	31	24	91	17

1985-86 SEASON

FIRST DIVISION

Liverpool	42	26	10	6	89	37	88
Everton	42	26	8	8	87	41	86
West Ham United	42	26	6	10	74	40	84
Manchester United	**42**	**22**	**10**	**10**	**70**	**36**	**76**
Sheffield Wednesday	42	21	10	11	63	54	73
Chelsea	42	20	11	11	57	56	71
Arsenal	42	20	9	13	49	47	69
Nottingham Forest	42	19	11	12	69	53	68
Luton Town	42	18	12	12	61	44	66
Tottenham Hotspur	42	19	8	15	74	52	65
Newcastle United	42	17	12	13	67	72	63
Watford	42	16	11	15	69	62	59
QPR	42	15	7	20	53	64	52
Southampton	42	12	10	20	51	62	46
Manchester City	42	11	12	19	43	57	45
Aston Villa	42	10	14	18	51	67	44
Coventry City	42	11	10	21	48	71	43
Oxford United	42	10	12	20	62	80	42
Leicester City	42	10	12	20	54	76	42
Ipswich Town	42	11	8	23	32	55	41
Birmingham City	42	8	5	29	30	73	29
West Brom	42	4	12	26	35	89	24

1986-87 SEASON

FIRST DIVISION

Everton	42	26	8	8	76	31	86
Liverpool	42	23	8	11	72	42	77
Tottenham Hotspur	42	21	8	13	68	43	71
Arsenal	42	20	10	12	58	35	70
Norwich City	42	17	17	8	53	51	68
Wimbledon	42	19	9	14	57	50	66
Luton Town	42	18	12	12	47	45	66
Nottingham Forest	42	18	11	13	64	51	65
Watford	42	18	9	15	67	54	63
Coventry City	42	17	12	13	50	45	63
Manchester United	**42**	**14**	**14**	**14**	**52**	**45**	**56**
Southampton	42	14	10	18	69	68	52
Sheffield Wednesday	42	13	13	16	58	59	52
Chelsea	42	13	13	16	53	64	52
West Ham United	42	14	10	18	52	67	52
QPR	42	13	11	18	48	64	50
Newcastle United	42	12	11	19	47	65	47
Oxford United	42	11	13	18	44	69	46
Charlton Athletic	42	11	11	20	45	55	44
Leicester City	42	11	9	22	54	76	42
Manchester City	42	8	15	19	36	57	39
Aston Villa	42	8	12	22	45	79	36

1987-88 SEASON

FIRST DIVISION

Liverpool	40	26	12	2	87	24	90
Manchester United	**40**	**23**	**12**	**5**	**71**	**38**	**81**
Nottingham Forest	40	20	13	7	67	39	73
Everton	40	19	13	8	53	27	70
QPR	40	19	10	11	48	38	67
Arsenal	40	18	12	10	58	39	66
Wimbledon	40	14	15	11	58	47	57
Newcastle United	40	14	14	12	55	53	56
Luton Town	40	14	11	15	57	58	53
Coventry City	40	13	14	13	46	53	53
Sheffield Wednesday	40	15	8	17	52	66	53
Southampton	40	12	14	14	49	53	50
Tottenham Hotspur	40	12	11	17	38	48	47
Norwich City	40	12	9	19	40	52	45
Derby County	40	10	13	17	35	45	43
West Ham United	40	9	15	16	40	52	42
Charlton Athletic	40	9	15	16	38	52	42
Chelsea	40	9	15	16	50	68	42
Portsmouth	40	7	14	19	36	66	35
Watford	40	7	11	22	27	51	32
Oxford United	40	6	13	21	44	80	31

1988-89 SEASON
FIRST DIVISION

Arsenal	38	22	10	6	73	36	76
Liverpool	38	22	10	6	65	28	76
Nottingham Forest	38	17	13	8	64	43	64
Norwich City	38	17	11	10	48	45	62
Derby County	38	17	7	14	40	38	58
Tottenham Hotspur	38	15	12	11	60	46	57
Coventry City	38	14	13	11	47	42	55
Everton	38	14	12	12	50	45	54
QPR	38	14	11	13	43	37	53
Millwall	38	14	11	13	47	52	53
Manchester United	**38**	**13**	**12**	**13**	**45**	**35**	**51**
Wimbledon	38	14	9	15	50	46	51
Southampton	38	10	15	13	52	66	45
Charlton Athletic	38	10	12	16	44	58	42
Sheffield Wednesday	38	10	12	16	34	51	42
Luton Town	38	10	11	17	42	52	41
Aston Villa	38	9	13	16	45	56	40
Middlesbrough	38	9	12	17	44	61	39
West Ham United	38	10	8	20	37	62	38
Newcastle United	38	7	10	21	32	63	31

1989-90 SEASON
FIRST DIVISION

Liverpool	38	23	10	5	78	37	79
Aston Villa	38	21	7	10	57	38	70
Tottenham Hotspur	38	19	6	13	59	47	63
Arsenal	38	18	8	12	54	38	62
Chelsea	38	16	12	10	58	50	60
Everton	38	17	8	13	51	33	59
Southampton	38	15	10	13	71	63	55
Wimbledon	38	13	16	9	47	40	55
Nottingham Forest	38	15	9	14	55	47	54
Norwich City	38	13	14	11	44	42	53
QPR	38	13	11	14	45	44	50
Coventry City	38	14	7	17	39	59	49
Manchester United	**38**	**13**	**9**	**16**	**46**	**47**	**48**
Manchester City	38	12	12	14	43	52	48
Crystal Palace	38	13	9	16	42	66	48
Derby County	38	13	7	18	43	40	46
Luton Town	38	10	13	15	43	57	43
Sheffield Wednesday	38	11	10	17	35	51	43
Charlton Athletic	38	7	9	22	31	57	30
Millwall	38	5	11	22	39	65	26

1990-91 SEASON
FIRST DIVISION

Arsenal	38	24	13	1	74	18	83
Liverpool	38	23	7	8	77	40	76
Crystal Palace	38	20	9	9	50	41	69
Leeds United	38	19	7	12	65	47	64
Manchester City	38	17	11	10	64	53	62
Manchester United	**38**	**16**	**12**	**10**	**58**	**45**	**59**
Wimbledon	38	14	14	10	53	46	56
Nottingham Forest	38	14	12	12	65	50	54
Everton	38	13	12	13	50	46	51
Tottenham	38	11	16	11	51	50	49
Chelsea	38	13	10	15	58	69	49
QPR	38	12	10	16	44	53	46
Sheffield United	38	13	7	18	36	55	46
Southampton	38	12	9	17	58	69	45
Norwich City	38	13	6	19	41	64	45
Coventry City	38	11	11	16	42	49	44
Aston Villa	38	9	14	15	46	58	41
Luton Town	38	10	7	21	42	61	37
Sunderland	38	8	10	20	38	60	34
Derby County	38	5	9	24	37	75	24

Arsenal 2 points deducted
Manchester United 1 point deducted

1991-92 SEASON
FIRST DIVISION

Leeds United	42	22	16	4	74	37	82
Manchester United	**42**	**21**	**15**	**6**	**63**	**33**	**78**
Sheffield Wednesday	42	21	12	9	62	49	75
Arsenal	42	19	15	8	81	46	72
Manchester City	42	20	10	12	61	48	70
Liverpool	42	16	16	10	47	40	64
Aston Villa	42	17	9	16	48	44	60
Nottingham Forest	42	16	11	15	60	58	59
Sheffield United	42	16	9	17	65	63	57
Crystal Palace	42	14	15	13	53	61	57
QPR	42	12	18	12	48	47	54
Everton	42	13	14	15	52	51	53
Wimbledon	42	13	14	15	53	53	53
Chelsea	42	13	14	15	50	60	53
Tottenham	42	15	7	20	58	63	52
Southampton	42	14	10	18	39	55	52
Oldham Athletic	42	14	9	19	63	67	51
Norwich City	42	11	12	19	47	63	45
Coventry City	42	11	11	20	35	44	44
Luton Town	42	10	12	20	38	71	42
Notts County	42	10	10	22	40	62	40
West Ham United	42	9	11	22	37	59	38

1992-93 SEASON

PREMIER DIVISION

Manchester United	42	24	12	6	67	31	84
Aston Villa	42	21	11	10	57	40	74
Norwich City	42	21	9	12	61	65	72
Blackburn Rovers	42	20	11	11	68	46	71
QPR	42	17	12	13	63	55	63
Liverpool	42	16	11	15	62	55	59
Sheffield Wednesday	42	15	14	13	55	51	59
Tottenham	42	16	11	15	60	66	59
Manchester City	42	15	12	15	56	51	57
Arsenal	42	15	11	16	40	38	56
Chelsea	42	14	14	14	51	54	56
Wimbledon	42	14	12	16	56	55	54
Everton	42	15	8	19	53	55	53
Sheffield United	42	14	10	18	54	53	52
Coventry City	42	13	13	16	52	57	52
Ipswich Town	42	12	16	14	50	55	52
Leeds United	42	12	15	15	57	62	51
Southampton	42	13	11	18	54	61	50
Oldham Athletic	42	13	10	19	63	74	49
Crystal Palace	42	11	16	15	48	61	49
Middlesbrough	42	11	11	20	54	75	44
Nottingham Forest	42	10	10	22	41	62	40

1993-94 SEASON

F.A. PREMIERSHIP

Manchester United	42	27	11	4	80	38	92
Blackburn Rovers	42	25	9	8	63	36	84
Newcastle United	42	23	8	11	82	41	77
Arsenal	42	18	17	7	53	28	71
Leeds United	42	18	16	8	65	39	70
Wimbledon	42	18	11	13	56	53	65
Sheffield Wednesday	42	16	16	10	76	54	64
Liverpool	42	17	9	16	59	55	60
QPR	42	16	12	14	62	64	60
Aston Villa	42	15	12	15	46	50	57
Coventry City	42	14	14	14	43	45	56
Norwich City	42	12	17	13	65	61	53
West Ham United	42	13	13	16	47	58	52
Chelsea	42	13	12	17	49	53	51
Tottenham Hotspur	42	11	12	19	54	59	45
Manchester City	42	9	18	15	38	49	45
Everton	42	12	8	22	42	63	44
Southampton	42	12	7	23	49	66	43
Ipswich Town	42	9	16	17	35	58	43
Sheffield United	42	8	18	16	42	60	42
Oldham Athletic	42	9	13	20	42	68	40
Swindon Town	42	5	15	22	47	100	30

No book about Manchester United would be complete without a picture of Bobby Charlton in action!

ALBISTON, Arthur

Edinburgh, 14th July 1957

Source	Season	Club	Apps.	Gls
App	1974-75	Manchester U	2	-
	1975-76		3	-
	1976-77		17	-
	1977-78		28	-
	1978-79		33	-
	1979-80		25	-
	1980-81		42	1
	1981-82		42	1
	1982-83		38	1
	1983-84		40	2
	1984-85		39	-
	1985-86		37	1
	1986-87		22	-
	1987-88		11	-
Tr	1988-89	West Brom A	43	2
Tr	1989-91	Dundee	10	-
Tr	1990-91	Chesterfield	3	1
Tr	1991-92	Chester C	44	
	1992-93		24	-

ANDERSON, Viv

Nottingham, 29th August 1956

Source	Season	Club	Apps.	Gls
App	1974-75	Nottingham F	16	-
	1975-76		21	-
	1976-77		38	1
	1977-78		37	3
	1978-79		40	1
	1979-80		41	3
	1980-81		31	-
	1981-82		39	-
	1982-83		25	1
	1983-84		40	6
Tr	1984-85	Arsenal	41	3
	1985-86		39	2
	1986-87		40	4
Tr	1987-88	Manchester U	31	2
	1988-89		6	-
	1989-90		16	-
	1990-91		1	-
Tr	1990-91	Sheffield W	22	2
	1991-92		22	3
	1992-93		26	3
Tr	1993-94	Barnsley	20	3

BAILEY, Gary

Ipswich, 9th August 1958

From Witts Univ., South Africa

Source	Season	Club	Apps.	Gls
	1977-78	Manchester U	-	-
	1978-79		28	-
	1979-80		42	-
	1980-81		40	-
	1981-82		39	-
	1982-83		37	-
	1983-84		40	-
	1984-85		38	-
	1985-86		25	-

Gary Bailey in action for United.

BARNES, Peter S.

Manchester, 10th June 1957

App	1974-75	Manchester C	3	1
	1975-76		28	3
	1976-77		21	2
	1977-78		34	8
	1978-79		29	1
Tr	1979-80	West Brom A	38	15
	1980-81		39	8
Tr	1981-82	Leeds U	30	1
From Real Betis (Spain)				
	1983-84	Leeds U	27	4
Tr	1984-85	Coventry C	18	2
Tr	1985-86	Manchester U	13	2
	1986-87		7	-
Tr	1986-87	Manchester C	8	-
Tr	1987-88	Hull C	11	-
Tr	1987-88	Manchester C	-	-
L	1987-88	Bolton W	2	-
L	1987-88	Port Vale	3	-
Tr	1988-89	Bolton W	3	-
Tr	1988-89	Sunderland	1	-

Steve Bruce, scored 13 goals during the 1990/91 Season.

BEARDSMORE, Russell

Wigan, 28th September 1968

App	1986-87	Manchester U	-	-
	1987-88		-	-
	1988-89		23	2
	1989-90		21	2
	1990-91		12	-
	1991-92		-	-
L	1991-92	Blackburn R	2	-
	1992-93	Manchester U	-	-
Tr	1993-94	Bournemouth	24	-

BLACKMORE, Clayton

Neath, 23rd September 1964

App	1982-83	Manchester U	-	-
	1983-84		1	-
	1984-85		1	-
	1985-86		12	3
	1986-87		12	1
	1987-88		22	3
	1988-89		28	3
	1989-90		28	2
	1990-91		35	4
	1991-92		33	3
	1992-93		14	-
	1993-94		-	-

BOSNICH, Mark

Fairfield, 13th January 1972

From Croatia Sydney

	1989-90	Manchester U	1	-
	1990-91		2	-
Tr	1991-92	Aston Villa	1	-
	1992-93		17	-
	1993-94		28	-

BRAZIL, Derek

Dublin, 14th December 1968

From Rivermont BC

	1985-86	Manchester U	-	-
	1986-87		-	-
	1987-88		-	-
	1988-89		1	-
	1989-90		1	-
	1990-91		-	-
L	1990-91	Oldham Ath	1	-
	1991-92	Manchester U	-	-
L	1991-92	Swansea C	12	1
Tr	1992-93	Cardiff C	34	-
	1993-94		31	-

BRUCE, Steve

Newcastle, 31st December 1960

App	1978-79	Gillingham	-	-
	1979-80		40	6
	1980-81		41	4

Source	Season	Club	Apps.	Gls
	1981-82		45	6
	1982-83		39	7
	1983-84		40	6
Tr	1984-85	Norwich C	39	1
	1985-86		42	8
	1986-87		41	3
	1987-88		19	2
Tr	1987-88	Manchester U	21	2
	1988-89		38	2
	1989-90		34	3
	1990-91		31	13
	1991-92		37	5
	1992-93		42	5
	1993-94		41	3

BUTT, Nicky

Manchester, 21st January 1975

Source	Season	Club	Apps.	Gls
YT	1992-93	Manchester U	1	-
	1993-94		1	-

CANTONA, Eric

Paris, 24th May 1966

From Nimes (France)

Source	Season	Club	Apps.	Gls
	1991-92	Leeds U	15	3
	1992-93		13	6
Tr	1992-93	Manchester U	22	9
	1993-94		34	18

DAVENPORT, Peter

Birkenhead, 24th March 1961

From Cammell Laird

Source	Season	Club	Apps.	Gls
	1981-82	Nottingham F	5	4
	1982-83		18	6
	1983-84		33	15
	1984-85		35	16
	1985-86		27	13
Tr	1985-86	Manchester U	11	1
	1986-87		39	14
	1987-88		34	5
	1988-89		8	2
Tr	1988-89	Middlesbrough	24	4
	1989-90		35	3
Tr	1990-91	Sunderland	29	7
	1991-92		36	4
	1992-93		34	4

DEMPSEY, Mark

Manchester, 14th January 1964

Source	Season	Club	Apps.	Gls
App	1981-82	Manchester U	-	-
	1982-83		-	-
	1983-84		-	-
	1984-85		-	-
L	1984-85	Swindon T	5	-
	1985-86	Manchester U	1	-
Tr	1986-87	Sheffield U	30	5
	1987-88		33	4
	1988-89		-	-

Source	Season	Club	Apps.	Gls
L	1988-89	Chesterfield	3	-
Tr	1988-89	Rotherham U	27	1
	1989-90		22	3
	1990-91		26	3

DONAGHY, Mal

Belfast, 13th September 1957

From Larne

Source	Season	Club	Apps.	Gls
	1978-79	Luton T	40	-
	1979-80		42	1
	1980-81		42	-
	1981-82		42	9
	1982-83		40	3
	1983-84		40	1
	1984-85		42	1
	1985-86		42	-
	1986-87		42	-
	1987-88		32	1
	1988-89		6	-
Tr	1988-89	Manchester U	30	-
	1989-90		14	-
L	1989-90	Luton T	5	-
	1990-91	Manchester U	25	-
	1991-92		20	-
Tr	1992-93	Chelsea	40	2
	1993-94		28	1

DUBLIN, Dion

Leicester, 22nd April 1969

Source	Season	Club	Apps.	Gls
	1987-88	Norwich C	-	-
Tr	1988-89	Cambridge U	21	6
	1989-90		46	15
	1990-91		46	16
	1991-92		43	15
Tr	1992-93	Manchester U	7	1
	1993-94		5	1

DUXBURY, Mike

Accrington, 1st September 1959

Source	Season	Club	Apps.	Gls
App	1976-77	Manchester U	-	-
	1977-78		-	-
	1978-79		-	-
	1979-80		-	-
	1980-81		33	2
	1981-82		24	-
	1982-83		42	1
	1983-84		39	-
	1984-85		30	1
	1985-86		23	1
	1986-87		32	1
	1987-88		39	-
	1988-89		18	-
	1989-90		19	-
Tr	1990-91	Blackburn R	22	-
	1991-92		5	-
Tr	1991-92	Bradford C	16	-
	1992-93		36	-
	1993-94		13	-

FERGUSON, Darren
Glasgow, 29th November 1972

Source	Season	Club	Apps.	Gls
YT	1990-91	Manchester U	5	-
	1991-92		4	-
	1992-93		15	-
	1993-94		3	-
Tr	1993-94	Wolverhampton W	14	-

GARTON, Billy
Salford, 15th March 1965

Source	Season	Club	Apps.	Gls
App	1982-83	Manchester U	-	-
	1983-84		-	-
	1984-85		2	-
	1985-86		10	-
L	1985-86	Birmingham C	5	-
	1986-87	Manchester U	9	-
	1987-88		6	-
	1988-89		14	-
	1989-90		-	-

GIBSON, Colin
Bridport, 6th April 1960

Source	Season	Club	Apps.	Gls
App	1977-78	Aston Villa	-	-
	1978-79		12	-
	1979-80		31	2
	1980-81		21	-
	1981-82		23	-
	1982-83		23	1
	1983-84		28	1
	1984-85		40	4
	1985-86		7	2
Tr	1985-86	Manchester U	18	5
	1986-87		24	1
	1987-88		29	2
	1988-89		2	-
	1989-90		6	1
	1990-91		-	-
L	1990-91	Port Vale	6	2
Tr	1990-91	Leicester C	18	1
	1991-92		17	3
	1992-93		9	-
	1993-94		15	-

GIBSON, Terry
Walthamstow, 23th December 1962

Source	Season	Club	Apps.	Gls
App	1979-80	Tottenham H	1	-
	1980-81		-	-
	1981-82		1	-
	1982-83		16	4
Tr	1983-84	Coventry C	36	17
	1984-85		38	15
	1985-86		24	11
Tr	1985-86	Manchester U	7	-
	1986-87		16	1
	1987-88		-	-
Tr	1987-88	Wimbledon	17	6
	1988-89		17	5

Source	Season	Club	Apps.	Gls
	1989-90		18	5
	1990-91		19	5
	1991-92		7	-
L	1991-92	Swindon T	9	1
	1992-93	Wimbledon	8	1
Tr	1993-94	Peterborough U	1	-
Tr	1993-94	Barnet	20	4

GIDMAN, John
Liverpool, 10th January 1954

From Liverpool Apprentice

Source	Season	Club	Apps.	Gls
	1971-72	Aston Villa	-	-
	1972-73		13	-
	1973-74		30	-
	1974-75		14	1
	1975-76		39	-
	1976-77		27	4
	1977-78		34	1
	1978-79		36	3
	1979-80		4	-
Tr	1979-80	Everton	29	1
	1980-81		35	1
Tr	1981-82	Manchester U	37	1
	1982-83		3	-
	1983-84		4	-
	1984-85		27	3
	1985-86		24	-
Tr	1986-87	Manchester C	22	-
	1987-88		31	1
Tr	1988-89	Stoke C	10	-
Tr	1988-89	Darlington	13	1

GIGGS, Ryan
Cardiff, 29th November 1973

From School

Source	Season	Club	Apps.	Gls
	1990-91	Manchester U	2	1
	1991-92		38	4
	1992-93		41	9
	1993-94		38	13

GILL, Tony
Bradford, 6th March 1968

Source	Season	Club	Apps.	Gls
App	1985-86	Manchester U	-	-
	1986-87		1	-
	1987-88		-	-
	1988-89		9	-
	1989-90		-	-

GRAHAM, Deiniol W. T.
Cannock, 4th October 1969

Source	Season	Club	Apps.	Gls
YT	1987-88	Manchester U	1	-
	1989-90		1	-
Tr	1991-92	Barnsley	21	1
	1992-93		15	1
L	1992-93	Preston NE	8	-
	1993-94	Barnsley	2	-
L	1993-94	Carlisle U	2	1

HIGGINS, Mark

Buxton, 29th September 1958

Source	Season	Club	Apps.	Gls
App	1976-77	Everton	2	-
	1977-78		26	1
	1978-79		21	1
	1979-80		19	-
	1980-81		2	-
	1981-82		29	3
	1982-83		39	1
	1983-84		14	-
Retired				
	1985-86	Manchester U	6	-
	1986-87		-	-
Tr	1986-87	Bury	22	-
	1987-88		41	-
	1988-89		5	-
Tr	1988-89	Stoke C	33	1
	1989-90		6	-

HOGG, Graeme

Aberdeen, 17th June 1964

Source	Season	Club	Apps.	Gls
App	1982-83	Manchester U	-	-
	1983-84		16	1
	1984-85		29	-
	1985-86		17	-
	1986-87		11	-
	1987-88		10	-
L	1987-88	West Brom A	7	-
Tr	1988-89	Portsmouth	41	1
	1989-90		39	1
	1990-91		20	-
Tr	1991-93	Hearts	57	3

HUGHES, Mark

Wrexham, 1st November 1963

Source	Season	Club	Apps.	Gls
App	1980-81	Manchester U	-	-
	1981-82		-	-
	1982-83		-	-
	1983-84		11	4
	1984-85		38	16
	1985-86		40	17
From Barcelona, Bayern Munich				
Tr	1988-89	Manchester U	38	14
	1989-90		37	13
	1990-91		31	10
	1991-92		39	11
	1992-93		41	15
	1993-94		36	11

INCE, Paul

Ilford, 21st October 1967

Source	Season	Club	Apps.	Gls
YT	1985-86	West Ham U	-	-
	1986-87		10	1
	1987-88		28	3
	1988-89		33	3
	1989-90		1	-
Tr	1989-90	Manchester U	26	-

Source	Season	Club	Apps.	Gls
	1990-91		31	3
	1991-92		33	3
	1992-93		41	6
	1993-94		39	8

IRWIN, Denis J.

Cork, 31st October 1965

Source	Season	Club	Apps.	Gls
App	1983-84	Leeds U	12	-
	1984-85		41	1
	1985-86		19	-
Tr	1986-87	Oldham A	41	1
	1987-88		43	-
	1988-89		41	2
	1989-90		42	1
Tr	1990-91	Manchester U	34	-
	1991-92		38	4
	1992-93		40	5
	1993-94		42	2

Denis Irwin, an ever-present for United during the 1993/94 Season.

Source	Season	Club	Apps.	Gls

KANCHELSKIS, Andrei

Kirowgrad, 23rd January 1969

From Dynamo Kiev, Donezts.

Source	Season	Club	Apps.	Gls
Tr	1990-91	Manchester U	1	-
	1991-92		34	5
	1992-93		27	3
	1993-94		31	6

KEANE, Roy

Cork, 10th August 1971

From Cobh Ramblers

Source	Season	Club	Apps.	Gls
Tr	1990-91	Nottingham F	35	8
	1991-92		39	8
	1992-93		40	6
Tr	1993-94	Manchester U	37	5

LEIGHTON, Jim

Johnstone, 24th July 1958

From Dalry Thistle

Source	Season	Club	Apps.	Gls
	1978-88	Aberdeen	302	-
Tr	1988-89	Manchester U	38	-
	1989-90		35	-
	1990-91		-	-
L	1990-91	Arsenal	-	-
	1991-92	Manchester U	-	-
L	1991-92	Reading	8	-
Tr	1991-93	Dundee	21	-
L	1992-93	Sheffield U	-	-
Tr	1993-94	Hibernian	44	-

McCLAIR, Brian

Bellshill, 8th December 1963

Source	Season	Club	Apps.	Gls
App	1980-81	Aston Villa	-	-
Tr	1981-83	Motherwell	39	15
Tr	1983-87	Celtic	145	99
Tr	1987-88	Manchester U	40	24
	1988-89		38	10
	1989-90		37	5
	1990-91		36	13
	1991-92		42	18
	1992-93		42	9
	1993-94		26	1

McGRATH, Paul

Greenford, 4th December 1959

From St. Patrick's Athletic

Source	Season	Club	Apps.	Gls
Tr	1981-82	Manchester U	-	-
	1982-83		14	3
	1983-84		9	1
	1984-85		23	-
	1985-86		40	3
	1986-87		35	2
	1987-88		22	2
	1988-89		20	1
Tr	1989-90	Aston Villa	35	1
	1990-91		35	-

Source	Season	Club	Apps.	Gls
	1991-92		41	1
	1992-93		42	4
	1993-94		30	1

McKEE, Colin

Glasgow, 22nd August 1973

Source	Season	Club	Apps.	Gls
YT	1991-92	Manchester U	-	-
	1992-93		-	-
L	1992-93	Bury	2	-
	1993-94	Manchester U	1	-

McQUEEN, Gordon

Kilburnie, 26th June 1952

Source	Season	Club	Apps.	Gls
	1970-73	St. Mirren	57	5
Tr	1972-73	Leeds U	6	-
	1973-74		36	-
	1974-75		33	2
	1975-76		10	1
	1976-77		34	7
	1977-78		21	5
Tr	1977-78	Manchester U	14	1
	1978-79		36	6
	1979-80		33	9
	1980-81		11	2
	1981-82		21	-
	1982-83		37	-
	1983-84		20	1

MAIORANA, Giuliano

Cambridge, 18th April 1969

From Histon

Source	Season	Club	Apps.	Gls
	1988-89	Manchester U	6	-
	1989-90		1	-
	1990-91		-	-
	1991-92		-	-

MARTIN, Lee

Hyde, 5th February 1968

Source	Season	Club	Apps.	Gls
	1986-87	Manchester U	-	-
	1987-88		1	-
	1988-89		24	-
	1989-90		32	1
	1990-91		14	-
	1991-92		1	-
	1992-93		-	-
	1993-94		1	-
Tr	1993-94	Celtic	15	-

MILNE, Ralph

Dundee, 13th May 1961

Source	Season	Club	Apps.	Gls
	1977-87	Dundee U	179	44
Tr	1986-87	Charlton Ath	12	-
	1987-88		10	-
Tr	1987-88	Bristol C	19	4
	1988-89		11	2
Tr	1988-89	Manchester U	22	3

Source	Season	Club	Apps.	Gls
	1989-90	....	1	-
L	1989-90	West Ham U................	-	-
	1990-91	Manchester U...............	-	-

MORAN, Kevin

Dublin, 29th April 1959

From Pegasus - Eire Gaelic Football

Source	Season	Club	Apps.	Gls
	1977-78	Manchester U...............	-	-
	1978-79	....	1	-
	1979-80	....	9	1
	1980-81	....	32	-
	1981-82	....	30	7
	1982-83	....	29	2
	1983-84	....	38	7
	1984-85	....	19	4
	1985-86	....	19	-
	1986-87	....	33	-
	1987-88	....	21	-

From Sporting Gijon

Source	Season	Club	Apps.	Gls
Tr	1989-90	Blackburn R................	19	2
	1990-91	....	32	1
	1991-92	....	41	2
	1992-93	....	36	4
	1993-94	....	19	1

MOSES, Remi

Manchester, 14th November 1960

Source	Season	Club	Apps.	Gls
App	1978-79	West Brom A................	-	-
	1979-80	....	18	1
	1980-81	....	41	4
	1981-82	....	4	-
Tr	1981-82	Manchester U...............	21	2
	1982-83	....	29	-
	1983-84	....	35	2
	1984-85	....	26	3
	1985-86	....	4	-

MUHREN, Arnold

Holland, 2nd June 1951

From FC Twente

Source	Season	Club	Apps.	Gls
Tr	1978-79	Ipswich T.....................	41	8
	1979-80	....	37	4
	1980-81	....	41	5
	1981-82	....	42	4
Tr	1982-83	Manchester U...............	32	5
	1983-84	....	26	8

NEVILLE, Gary

Bury, 18th February 1975

Source	Season	Club	Apps.	Gls
YT	1992-93	Manchester U...............	-	-
	1993-94	....	1	-

O'BRIEN, William F. (Liam)

Dublin, 5th September 1964

From Shamrock Rovers

Source	Season	Club	Apps.	Gls
	1986-87	Manchester U...............	11	-

Gary Pallister, Manchester United and England defender.

Source	Season	Club	Apps.	Gls
	1987-88	....	17	2
	1988-89	....	3	-
Tr	1988-89	Newcastle U................	20	4
	1989-90	....	19	2
	1990-91	....	33	3
	1991-92	....	40	4
	1992-93	....	33	6
	1993-94	....	6	-
Tr	1993-94	Tranmere R	17	1

OLSEN, Jesper

Fakse, 20th March 1961

From Naestved and Ajax

Source	Season	Club	Apps.	Gls
Tr	1984-85	Manchester U................	36	5
	1985-86	....	28	11
	1986-87	....	28	3
	1987-88	....	37	2
	1988-89	....	10	-

To Bordeaux

Source	Season	Club	Apps.	Gls

PALLISTER, Gary

Ramsgate, 30th June 1965

Source	Season	Club	Apps.	Gls
	1984-85	Middlesbrough	-	-
	1985-86		28	-
L	1985-86	Darlington	7	-
	1986-87	Middlesbrough	44	1
	1987-88		44	3
	1988-89		37	1
	1989-90		3	-
Tr	1989-90	Manchester U	35	3
	1990-91		36	-
	1991-92		40	1
	1992-93		42	1
	1993-94		41	1

PARKER, Paul

Essex, 4th April 1964

Source	Season	Club	Apps.	Gls
App	1980-81	Fulham	1	-
	1981-82		5	-
	1982-83		16	-
	1983-84		34	-
	1984-85		36	-
	1985-86		30	-
	1986-87		31	2
Tr	1987-88	QPR	40	-
	1988-89		36	-
	1989-90		32	-
	1990-91		17	1
Tr	1991-92	Manchester U	26	-
	1992-93		31	1
	1993-94		40	-

PEARS, Steve

Brandon, 22nd January 1962

Source	Season	Club	Apps.	Gls
App	1978-79	Manchester U	-	-
	1979-80		-	-
	1980-81		-	-
	1981-82		-	-
	1982-83		-	-
	1983-84		-	-
L	1983-84	Middlesbrough	12	-
	1984-85	Manchester U	4	-
Tr	1985-86	Middlesbrough	38	-
	1986-87		46	-
	1987-88		43	-
	1988-89		26	-
	1989-90		25	-
	1990-91		27	-
	1991-92		45	-
	1992-93		26	-
	1993-94		46	-

PHELAN, Mike

Nelson, 24th September 1962

Source	Season	Club	Apps.	Gls
App	1980-81	Burnley	16	2
	1981-82		23	1
	1982-83		42	3

Source	Season	Club	Apps.	Gls
	1983-84		44	2
	1984-85		43	1
Tr	1985-86	Norwich C	42	3
	1986-87		40	4
	1987-88		37	-
	1988-89		37	2
Tr	1989-90	Manchester U	38	1
	1990-91		33	1
	1991-92		18	-
	1992-93		11	-
	1993-94		2	-

ROBINS, Mark

Ashton-under-Lyme, 22nd December 1969

Source	Season	Club	Apps.	Gls
App	1986-87	Manchester U	-	-
	1987-88		-	-
	1988-89		10	-
	1989-90		17	7
	1990-91		19	4
	1991-92		2	-
Tr	1992-93	Norwich C	37	15
	1993-94		13	1

ROBSON, Bryan

Chester-le-Street, 11th January 1957

Source	Season	Club	Apps.	Gls
App	1974-75	West Brom A	3	2
	1975-76		16	1
	1976-77		23	8
	1977-78		35	3
	1978-79		41	7
	1979-80		34	8
	1980-81		40	10
	1981-82		5	-
Tr	1981-82	Manchester U	32	5
	1982-83		33	10
	1983-84		33	12
	1984-85		33	9
	1985-86		21	7
	1986-87		30	7
	1987-88		36	11
	1988-89		34	4
	1989-90		20	2
	1990-91		17	1
	1991-92		27	4
	1992-93		14	1
	1993-94		15	1

SCHMEICHEL, Peter

Glodsone, 18th November 1968

From Hvidovre and Brondby

Source	Season	Club	Apps.	Gls
Tr	1991-92	Manchester U	40	-
	1992-93		42	-
	1993-94		40	-

SEALEY, Les

Bethnal Green, 29th September 1957

Source	Season	Club	Apps.	Gls
App	1975-76	Coventry C	-	-

| --- | --- | --- | --- | --- |
	1976-77		11	-
	1977-78		2	-
	1978-79		36	-
	1979-80		20	-
	1980-81		35	-
	1981-82		15	-
	1982-83		39	-
Tr	1983-84	Luton T	42	-
	1984-85		26	-
L	1984-85	Plymouth Arg	6	-
	1985-86	Luton T	35	-
	1986-87		41	-
	1987-88		31	-
	1988-89		32	-
	1989-90		-	-
L	1989-90	Manchester U	2	-
Tr	1990-91	Manchester U	31	-
Tr	1991-92	Aston Villa	18	-
L	1991-92	Coventry C	2	-
	1992-93	Aston Villa	-	-
L	1992-93	Birmingham C	12	-
	1992-93	Manchester U	-	-
	1993-94		-	-

SHARPE, Lee
Halesowen, 25th July 1971

Source	Season	Club	Apps.	Gls
YT	1987-88	Torquay U	13	3
Tr	1988-89	Manchester U	22	-
	1989-90		18	1
	1990-91		23	2
	1991-92		14	1
	1992-93		27	1
	1993-94		30	9

SIVEBAEK, John
Vejle, 25th October 1961

From Vejle

Source	Season	Club	Apps.	Gls
Tr	1985-86	Manchester U	3	-

STAPLETON, Frank
Dublin, 10th July 1956

Source	Season	Club	Apps.	Gls
App	1973-74	Arsenal	-	-
	1974-75		1	-
	1975-76		25	4
	1976-77		40	13
	1977-78		39	13
	1978-79		41	17
	1979-80		39	14
	1980-81		40	14
Tr	1981-82	Manchester U	41	13
	1982-83		41	14
	1983-84		42	13
	1984-85		24	6
	1985-86		41	7
	1986-87		34	7
Tr	1987-88	Ajax	4	-
Tr	1987-88	Derby Co	10	1
From Le Havre				
Tr	1989-90	Blackburn R	43	3

Source	Season	Club	Apps.	Gls
	1990-91		38	10
Tr	1991-92	Aldershot	1	-
Tr	1991-92	Huddersfield T	5	-
Tr	1991-92	Bradford C	27	-
	1992-93		13	2
	1993-94		28	-

STRACHAN, Gordon D.
Edinburgh, 9th February 1957

Source	Season	Club	Apps.	Gls
App	1974-77	Dundee	60	13
Tr	1977-84	Aberdeen	183	70
Tr	1984-85	Manchester U	41	15
	1985-86		28	5
	1986-87		34	4
	1987-88		36	8
	1988-89		21	1
Tr	1988-89	Leeds U	11	3
	1989-90		46	16
	1990-91		34	7
	1991-92		36	4
	1992-93		31	4
	1993-94		33	3

THORNLEY, Ben
Bury, 21st April 1975

Source	Season	Club	Apps.	Gls
YT	1992-93	Manchester U	-	-
	1993-94		1	-

TURNER, Christopher R.
Sheffield, 15th September 1958

Source	Season	Club	Apps.	Gls
App	1976-77	Sheffield W	45	-
	1977-78		23	-
	1978-79		23	-
L	1978-79	Lincoln C	5	-
Tr	1979-80	Sunderland	30	-
	1980-81		27	-
	1981-82		19	-
	1982-83		35	-
	1983-84		42	-
	1984-85		42	-
Tr	1985-86	Manchester U	17	-
	1986-87		23	-
	1987-88		24	-
Tr	1988-89	Sheffield W	29	-
	1989-90		23	-
L	1989-90	Leeds U	2	-
	1990-91	Sheffield W	23	-
Tr	1991-92	Leyton Orient	34	-
	1992-93		17	-
	1993-94		6	-

WALLACE, Danny
London, 21st January 1964

Source	Season	Club	Apps.	Gls
App	1980-81	Southampton	2	-
	1981-82		7	-
	1982-83		35	12
	1983-84		41	11

Source	Season	Club	Apps.	Gls
	1984-85	....	35	7
	1985-86	....	35	8
	1986-87	....	31	8
	1987-88	....	33	11
	1988-89	....	31	5
	1989-90	....	5	2
Tr	1989-90	Manchester U	26	3
	1990-91	....	19	3
	1991-92	....	-	-
	1992-93	....	2	-
L	1992-93	Millwall	3	-
	1993-94	Manchester U	-	-
Tr	1993-94	Birmingham C	10	1

WALSH, Gary
Wigan, 21st March 1968

Source	Season	Club	Apps.	Gls
	1984-85	Manchester U	-	-
	1985-86	....	-	-
	1986-87	....	14	-
	1987-88	....	16	-
	1988-89	....	-	-
L	1988-89	Airdrie	3	-
	1989-90	Manchester U	-	-
	1990-91	....	5	-
	1991-92	....	2	-
	1992-93	....	-	-
	1993-94	....	3	-
L	1993-94	Oldham Ath	6	-

WEBB, Neil
Reading, 30th July 1963

Source	Season	Club	Apps.	Gls
App	1979-80	Reading	5	-
	1980-81	....	27	7
	1981-82	....	40	15
Tr	1982-83	Portsmouth	42	8
	1983-84	....	40	10
	1984-85	....	41	16
Tr	1985-86	Nottingham F	38	14
	1986-87	....	32	14
	1987-88	....	40	13
	1988-89	....	36	6
Tr	1989-90	Manchester U	11	2
	1990-91	....	32	3
	1991-92	....	31	3
	1992-93	....	1	-
Tr	1992-93	Nottingham F	9	-
	1993-94	....	21	3

WHITESIDE, Norman
Belfast, 7th May 1965

Source	Season	Club	Apps.	Gls
App	1981-82	Manchester U	2	1
	1982-83	....	39	8
	1983-84	....	37	10
	1984-85	....	27	9
	1985-86	....	37	4
	1986-87	....	31	8
	1987-88	....	27	7
	1988-89	....	6	-
Tr	1989-90	Everton	27	9

Source	Season	Club	Apps.	Gls
	1990-91	....	2	-

WHITWORTH, Neil
Ince, 12th April 1972

Source	Season	Club	Apps.	Gls
YT	1989-90	Wigan Ath	2	-
Tr	1990-91	Manchester U	1	-
	1991-92		-	-
L	1991-92	Preston NE..................	6	-
L	1991-92	Barnsley......................	11	-

WILSON, David
Burnley, 20th March 1969

Source	Season	Club	Apps.	Gls
App	1986-87	Manchester U	-	-
	1987-88	....	-	-
	1988-89	....	4	-
	1989-90	....	-	-
	1990-91	....	-	-
L	1990-91	Charlton Ath................	7	2
L	1990-91	Lincoln C....................	3	-
Tr	1991-92	Bristol R	3	-
	1992-93	....	8	-

WOOD, Nicky
Oldham, 11th January 1966

From School

Source	Season	Club	Apps.	Gls
	1983-84	Manchester U	-	-
	1984-85	....	-	-
	1985-86	....	1	-
	1986-87	....	2	-
	1987-88	....	-	-
	1988-89	....	-	-

WRATTEN, Paul
Middlesbrough, 29th November 1970

Source	Season	Club	Apps.	Gls
YT	1988-89	Manchester U	-	-
	1989-90	....	-	-
	1990-91	....	2	-
	1991-92	....	-	-
Tr	1992-93	Hartlepool U................	15	1
	1993-94	....	42	-

New title also available in The 10 Seasons Series: -

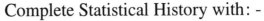
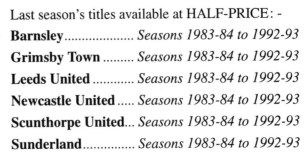
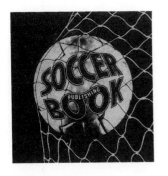

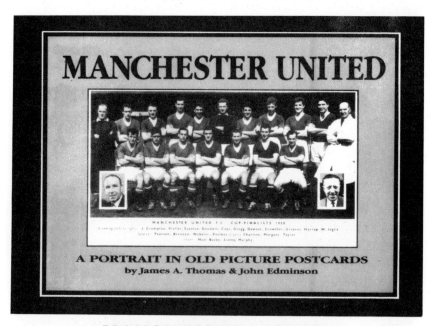

MANCHESTER UNITED -
A PORTRAIT IN OLD PICTURE POSTCARDS.

A fascinating book tracing the history of United in old postcards.
80 pages featuring postcards from 1903 to 1969.

Excellent value at £6.50 per copy + £1.00 postage

SPECIAL OFFER:

This book available for only £3.50 + postage when purchased with
Busby - Epitaph to a Legend (see opposite page).

(see opposite page).

Order From : - **THE SOCCER BOOKSHELF
DEPT. M10S
72 ST. PETERS AVENUE
CLEETHORPES
SOUTH HUMBERSIDE
DN35 8HU**

BUSBY - EPITAPH TO A LEGEND.
by Stan Liversedge.

The inside story of Sir Matt and Manchester United. Excellent value with 144 pages and over 30 photos.

Softback Price £5.99 per copy + 50p postage

(See opposite for ordering information and Special Offer)

Supporters' Guides : -

THE SUPPORTERS' GUIDE TO PREMIER & FOOTBALL LEAGUE CLUBS 1995

Featuring :
- all F.A. Carling Premiership clubs
- all Football League clubs
+ Results, tables

112 pages - price £4.99 - post free

THE SUPPORTERS' GUIDE TO NON-LEAGUE FOOTBALL 1995

Featuring :
- all GM/Vauxhall Conference clubs
- all Northern Premier clubs
- all Beazer Homes - Premier clubs
- all Diadora Premier clubs
+ 180 other major Non-League clubs

112 pages - price £4.99 - post free

THE SUPPORTERS' GUIDE TO SCOTTISH FOOTBALL 1995

Featuring :
- all Scottish League clubs
- all Highland League clubs
- all East & South of Scotland League clubs
+ Results, tables

96 pages - price £4.99 - post free

THE SUPPORTERS' GUIDE TO WELSH FOOTBALL 1995

order from : -

SOCCER BOOK PUB. LTD.
DEPT. SBP
72 ST. PETERS AVENUE
CLEETHORPES
DN35 8HU
ENGLAND

Featuring :
- all Konica League of Wales clubs
- all Cymru Alliance clubs
- all Welsh Football League clubs
+ 'The Exiles', Minor League clubs & 1993/94
season's results and tables

96 pages - price £4.99 - post free